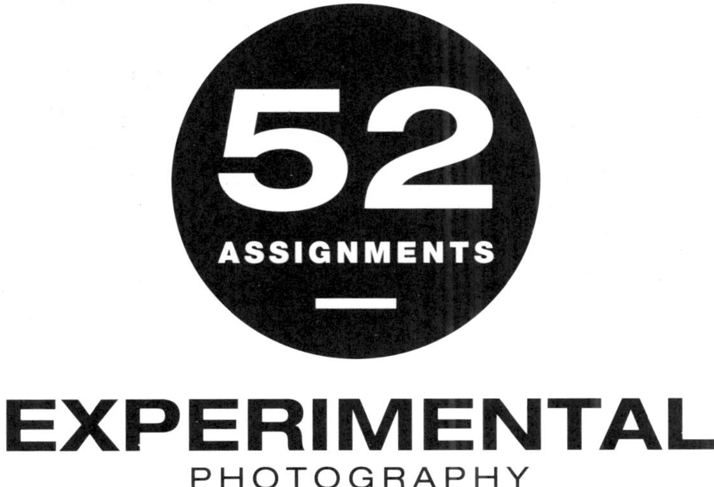

EXPERIMENTAL
PHOTOGRAPHY

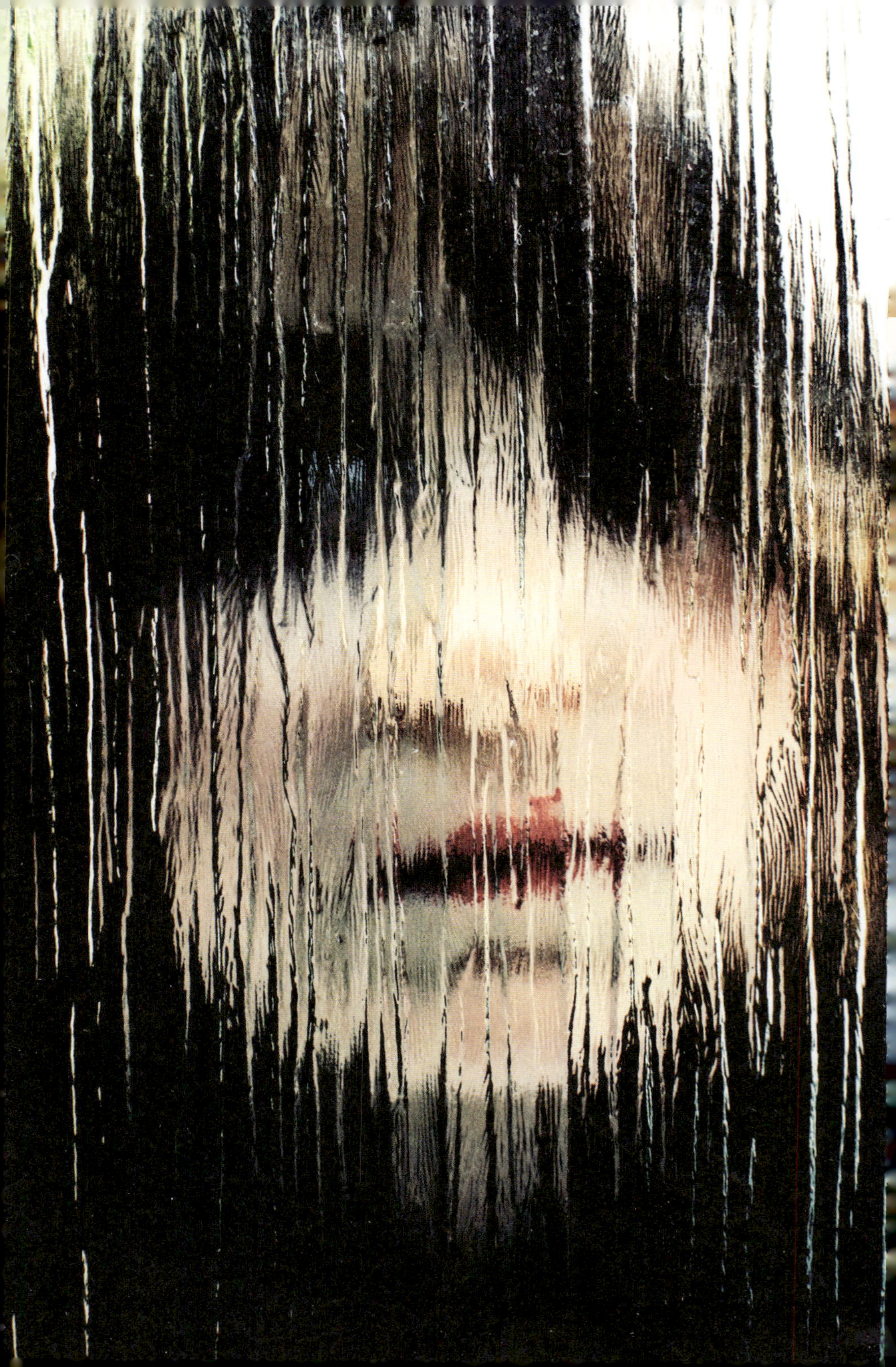

52 ASSIGNMENTS

EXPERIMENTAL
PHOTOGRAPHY

CHRIS GATCUM

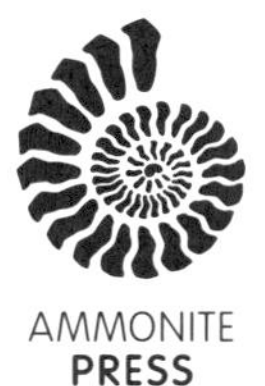

AMMONITE
PRESS

ASSIGNMENTS

Tick off your completed projects

ASSIGNMENT KEY

Each assignment has symbols showing the type of tasks involved.

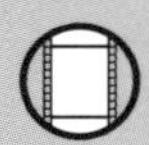 FILM

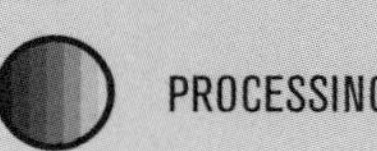 PROCESSING

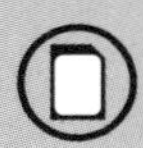 DIGITAL

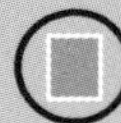 PRINTING

ASSIGNMENT JOURNAL

Use the journal spaces throughout the book to keep a record of your experimental assignments and images.

INTRODUCTION

Some people insist photography is an art. Others are adamant it's a science. I'd suggest it's more than both of those things: I'd say it's *fun*.

It doesn't matter what camera you first pick up, or what you want to photograph with it: everyone is a complete novice when they start out. We're not artists or scientists, we're enthusiastic children embarking on an exploration of the world through a lens, making basic mistakes and taking some spectacularly dreadful pictures along the way. Making pictures is magical, the results are intoxicating, and the whole process one is great big exciting adventure.

And then we grow up...

Our photography matures and our growing proficiency leads to an increasingly clinical approach. Where once there was spontaneity, frivolity, and a devil-may-care approach, we now find ourselves trying to recall rules, formulas, and the most appropriate workflow for any given situation. This may show that we have "mastered" the subject, but there's a very real risk at this stage that our pictures will become stale and homogenous as a result, and—worse—that we'll fall out of love with photography. I know because it happened to me.

Thankfully, you've bought this book (or are at least thinking about it), so you've already taken the first step toward stopping the creative rot. Within its pages are 52 photo-related assignments designed to unlock the shackles of mundanity and kickstart your creativity. Some of the experiments involve film, some are digitally based, some are about printing or processing, and others enter the realm of camera and lens hacks. There are no chapters, no neatly pigeon-holed ideas, and no notion of right and wrong—everything and anything goes, and it's entirely up to you how you approach it.

You may not want to try all the assignments, or you might decide to try everything once—it really doesn't matter. What matters most is that you try something new. So make a lens, abuse some film, think about "losing focus", or combine multiple experiments and see what happens when you push your photography in a different direction.

Above all, have fun!

Chris Gatcum

KIT LIST

- Camera with manual focus control

TIPS

- You can defocus your images to the point that they become unrecognizable abstracts; or soften them a little less aggressively, so they are still "readable."

- Depth of field affects how much of a scene appears "sharp," which in turn determines how far you need to defocus to get the look you're after.

SEE ALSO

Japanese photographer Hiroshi Sugimoto takes "unfocusing" to a whole new level by using a modified camera that focuses beyond infinity.

LOSING FOCUS

A lot of people talk about getting things "in focus" as if it's mandatory; but, like most things in photography, it's entirely optional. There's no law that says your subject (or even your entire shot) must be in focus, so switch your camera to manual focus and set the sharpest point in front of your subject, behind it, or defocus the image entirely.

ASSIGNMENT JOURNAL

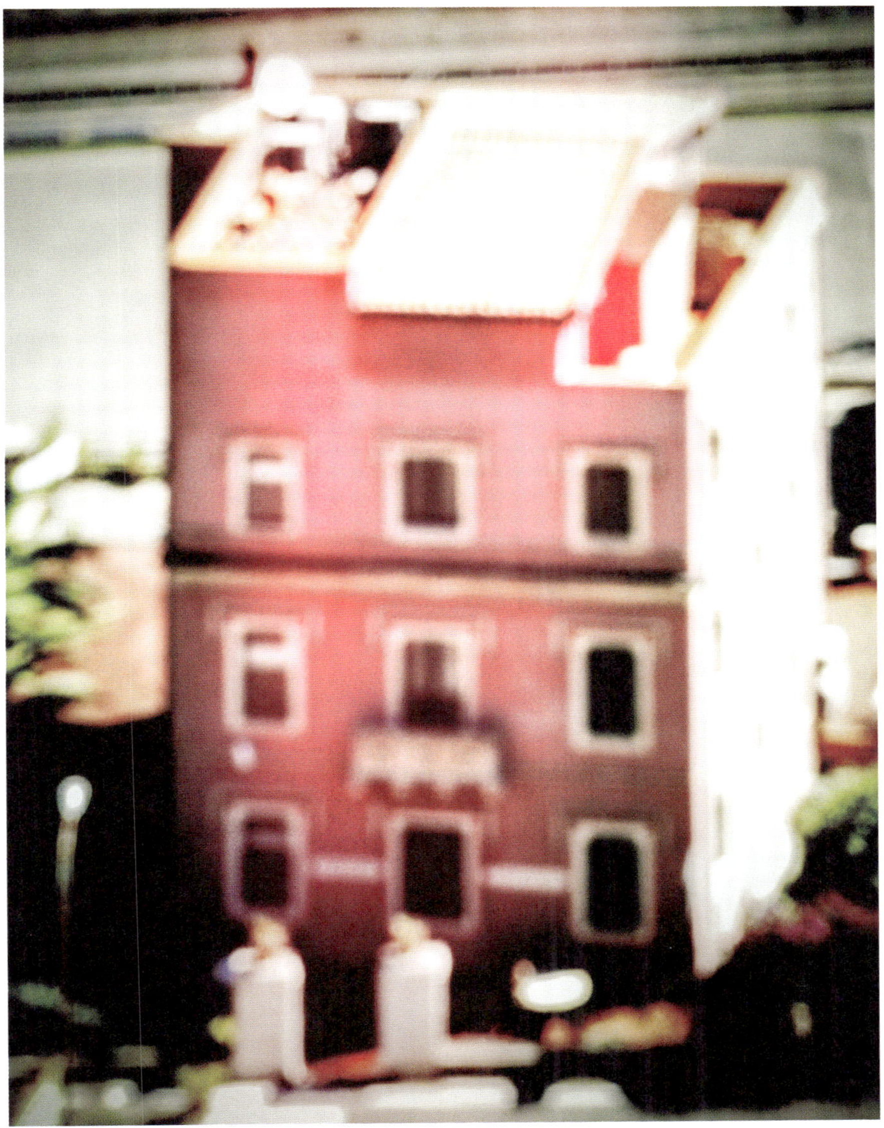

▲ *"Unfocus" any shot you like, but it can help the viewer if something about it remains recognizable. Although this picture isn't focused it still "reads" as a house.*

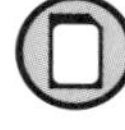
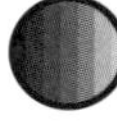
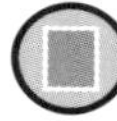

KIT LIST

- Digital image
- The Rasterbator software (rasterbator.net)

TIPS

The Rasterbator is available in two (free!) versions: online and standalone. The online version is the one to use as it benefits from the latest developments and is also multiplatform. The only (very slight) downside is that it has a maximum image output size of 1,000 pages. That's more than enough for most people, but the Windows-only standalone version offers an unlimited output size for truly gargantuan prints.

SEE ALSO

- If you switch to "No effects" output (rather than "Rasterbation" mode), The Rasterbator can be used to create "joiners," as you'll see in Assignment 22.

- Shooting the image on a TV screen (Assignment 05) will create a similar dot image.

RASTERBATE

There's no denying that big prints rock! Putting the photographic results of your experiments in an album or journal is great, but nothing beats seeing one of your prize images taking up a whole load of wall real estate. Of course, getting large prints made can be expensive—unless, that is, you "rasterbate."

Since 2004 a simple cult program known as The Rasterbator has been helping photographers enlarge their images to truly gargantuan sizes that can be printed on a regular desktop printer. The magic lies in algorithms that transform a digital image

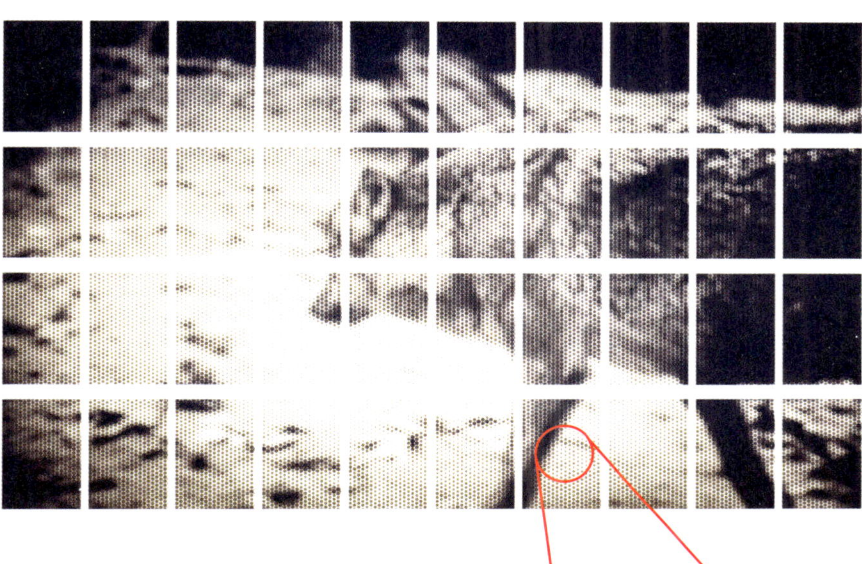

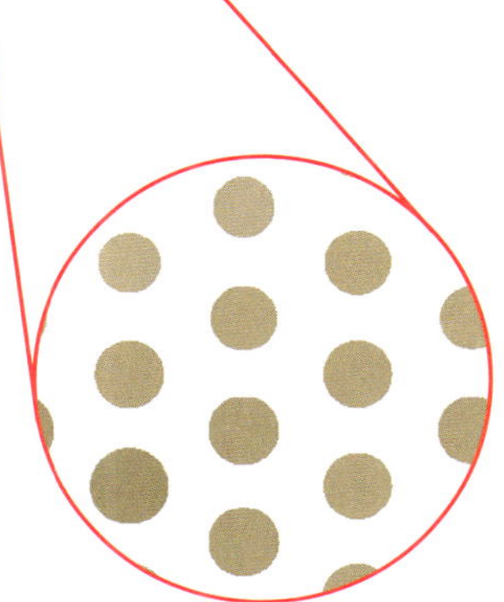

▲ *The Rasterbator's impressionistic images are a result of transforming photographs into dots that can be scaled by impressively high amounts. For example, each of the panels in this shot of a wolf measures 8x12 inches (A4), which combine to produce a wall-filling image that's approximately 80x48 inches (2x1.2m) in size.*

from a regular grid of pixels to Impressionist-style dots that can be enlarged to virtually any size. The Rasterbator will then tile the enlarged image across multiple pages that you can print out on a regular desktop inkjet or laser printer, turning the smallest image into a multi-page billboard poster!

Multiple options in the software let you change the raster (dot) pattern or disable it completely, print with or without borders, set the output size, and much, much more—so you can really go wild with your experiments!

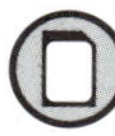

KIT LIST

• Camera with shutter speed control

SEE ALSO

If you like to add motion blur to your shots, there are plenty of options for you, including panning (Assignment 09), camera tossing (Assignment 07), and zoom bursts (Assignment 13), each of which creates unique results.

TIPS

• There's no benefit to using the viewfinder, as you're not going to see what the camera records. Instead, aim the camera and "shoot blind" for added unpredictability.

• You can avoid reflections by rolling down your window to shoot, but make sure you've got a good grip on your camera.

• Shooting in urban areas at night combines abstract blurs with light trails.

• Don't shoot and drive! Only use your camera if you're in the passenger seat.

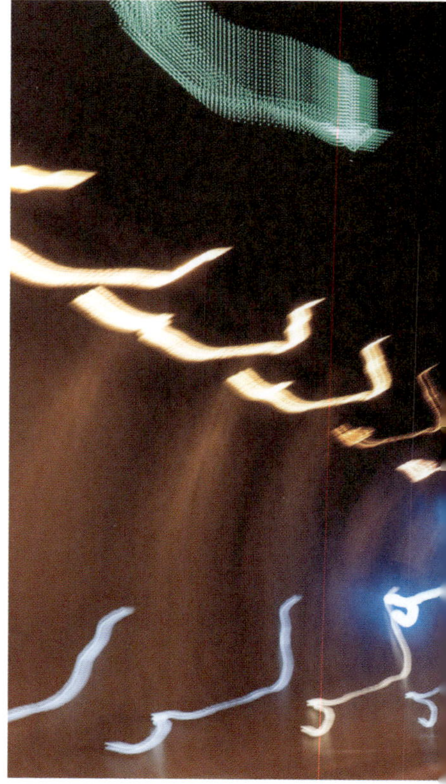

DRIVE-BY SHOOTING

Moving your camera while you take a photograph is usually something you'd want to avoid, but take it to extremes and you can create some great abstract images. All you need to do is get yourself in a car, bus, train—or any other moving vehicle—and shoot with a slow shutter speed. The slower the shutter speed, the more blurred the result.

If you want to get technical, your focal length and the vehicle speed will both impact on the result as well, so you may want to experiment to find the "best" shutter speed: use Shutter Priority to set a specific exposure time.

▼ *This "drive-by" shot was taken from the passenger seat of a RV while driving through a tunnel in Spain. The shutter speed used here was 1.5 sec., which was largely dictated by the tunnel's dark interior.*

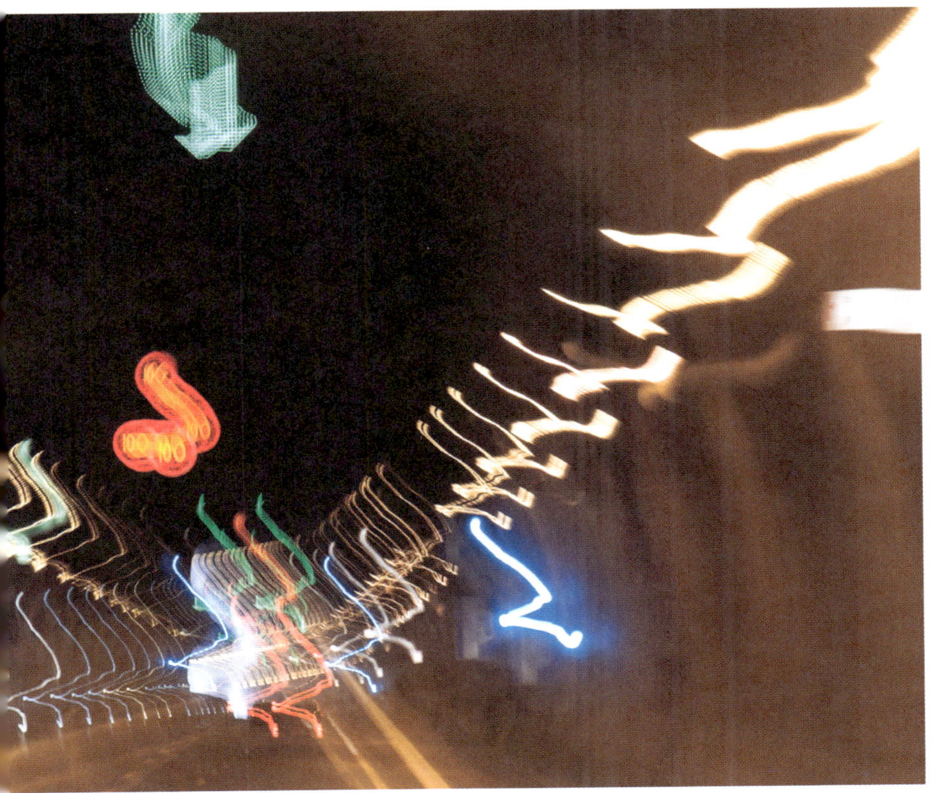

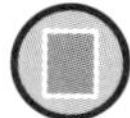

ASSIGNMENT

04

KIT LIST

- Inkjet printer
- Label backing paper (or acetate sheets)
- Paper, card, or other surface on which to transfer the image
- Small roller (optional)

TIPS

- Experiment with different receiving media; absorbent surfaces generally work best as they allow the ink to soak in.

- The transferred image will not have the same level of detail as the original photo, so choose your shots carefully—graphic photos tend to work better than detail-packed images.

- Try to avoid "smearing" your wet print as you place it down, otherwise you'll smudge your image.

SEE ALSO

- No inkjet printer? No problem! You can transfer images made using a laser printer or color copier—just flip to Assignment 45.

- Why not try combining your inkjet transfers with other techniques, such as multi-shot joiners (Assignments 22 and 23)?

ASSIGNMENT JOURNAL

INKJET TRANSFER

Your inkjet printer can make pixel-perfect reproductions of your photographs, but did you know that it can also help you to create one-off masterpieces in the form of "transfer" images?

Normally when you make a print, the tiny droplets of ink are absorbed by the specialist coatings on your photo-quality paper (or the paper itself), and dry almost instantly. However, if you print on a material that doesn't absorb the ink, your print won't dry immediately, so you can transfer the liquid image to a different surface that your printer wouldn't otherwise be able to handle!

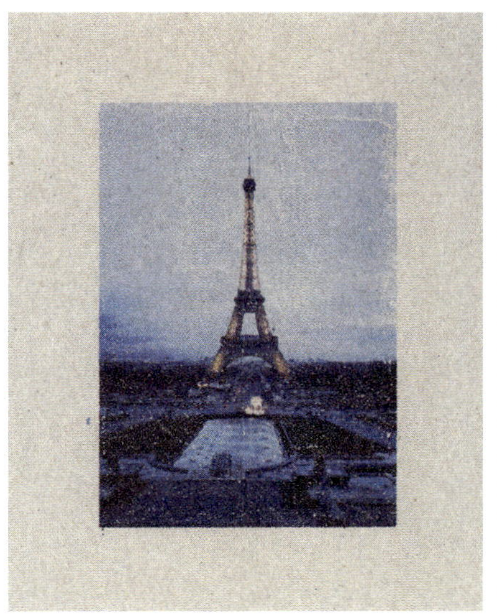
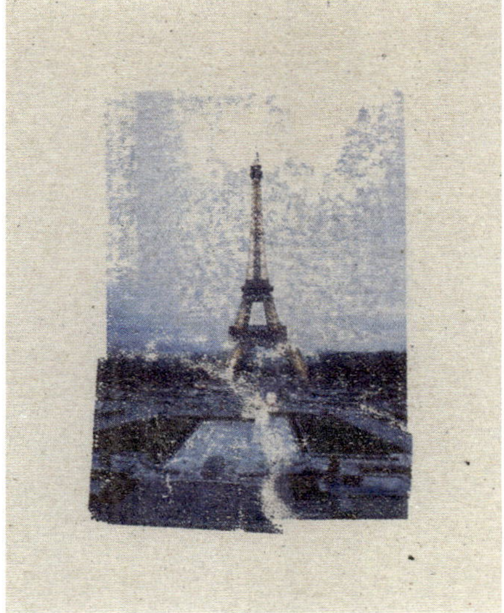

▲ *No two inkjet transfers are the same: this is the same start image, which went through the same transfer process to the same receiving medium (heavy, gray card stock), but the results are very different.*

THE PROCESS

1 One of the best media for inkjet transfers is the waxy backing paper that adhesive labels usually come on. Just remove the sticky labels and you're good to go. You can also use acetate sheets, but you need to make sure this is regular acetate, not the type designed for inkjet printers—you don't want the ink to be "accepted" by the medium.

2 Open your image in your editing software. The transfer process will reverse the image, so you'll need to flip your photo before you print it (so it transfers the "right way round"). This is especially important if you've got writing in your shot.

3 With most printers you'll need to manually load your transfer medium one sheet at a time, rather than stacking it in a paper tray. If you're using label backing paper, make sure the waxy side is the one you'll be printing on.

4 You'll have to experiment with your print quality settings to find the ones that work best for you, but as you want to get plenty of ink to transfer, choosing "Glossy Photo Paper" is a good start point. Hit "Print" when you're done.

5 When your print rolls out of your printer it won't be dry, so you will need to handle it with care. Take your wet print and carefully place it ink-side down on your receiving medium (your paper, card, wood, or whatever surface you're transferring your image to).

6 Using a rubber roller (available from most craft stores) or the side of your hand, apply gentle pressure across the back of your transfer medium to transfer the ink to the new surface.

7 Carefully peel the backing paper off to reveal your transferred masterpiece!

ASSIGNMENT JOURNAL

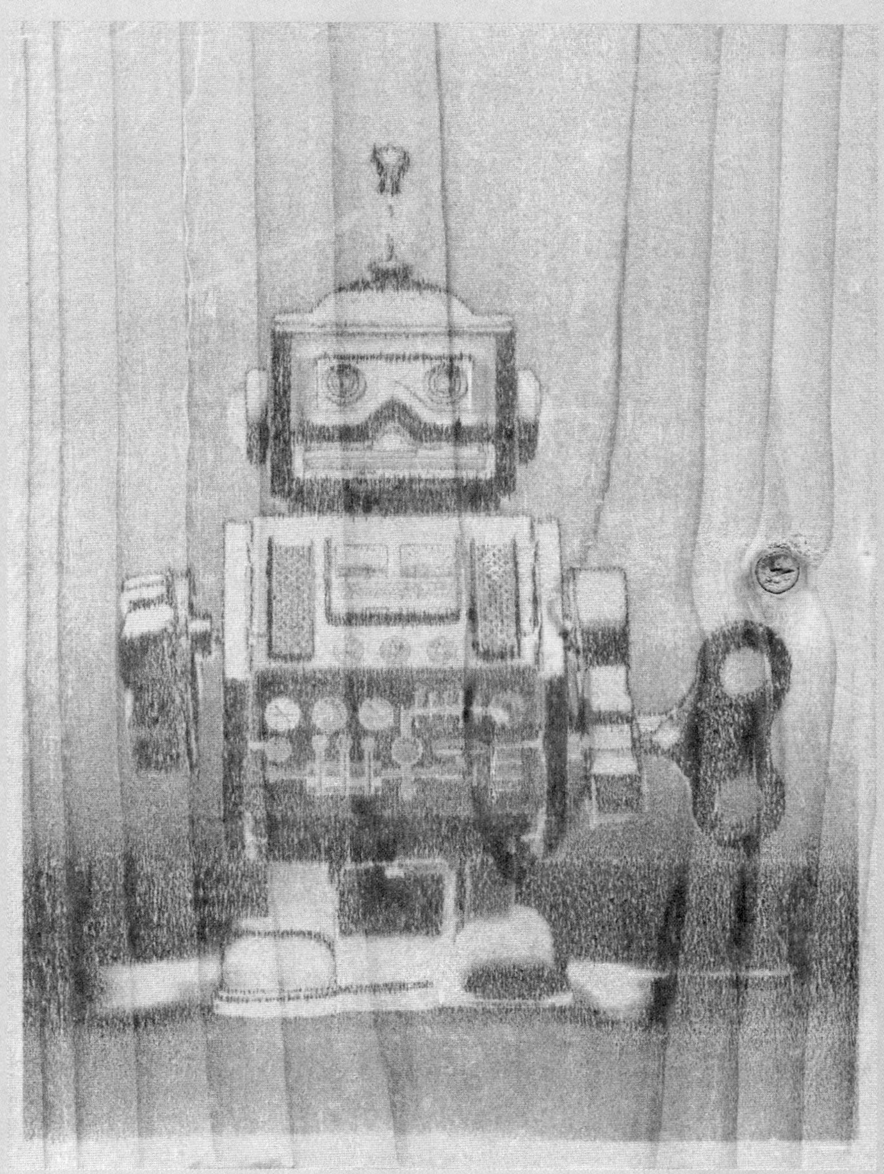

▲ *Although you can transfer your images to textured papers and card, experiment with other surfaces as well—wood is naturally absorbent, so it's well worth trying.*

KIT LIST

- Any type of camera (including cameraphone)
- Digital image
- Computer monitor or TV

TIPS

- Shoot at an angle with a wide aperture to selectively focus part of the on-screen image, or photograph straight-on with a smaller aperture to keep everything sharp.

- Vary your shooting distance to vary the size of the dot pattern—the closer you get to the screen, the more apparent the screen pattern will be.

- Moiré can be more of an issue if you're using a digital camera without an anti-aliasing filter.

SEE ALSO

The dot-screen effect can also be seen when you use The Rasterbator to process and print your images in Assignment 02.

SCREEN STAR

Rephotographing an image displayed on a television or computer monitor is a great way of adding a bit of texture to your shot, especially if you use an older CRT monitor or television (the ones with a "big back"). Modern flat screens will also work, but the images you'll get are a whole lot "cleaner"—the old-school tech gives a more vintage vibe and can also start to introduce some great distortions, courtesy of the bulging, heavy-glass screen. However, you will need to work a bit harder to get your images on the screen of an older display, and might have to track down some obscure adaptors or cables.

In both cases, the process is the same: you get your image up on screen, set up your camera, dim the lights (to avoid any reflections), and photograph the screen to recapture your picture in all its dot-based (or pixel-based) glory.

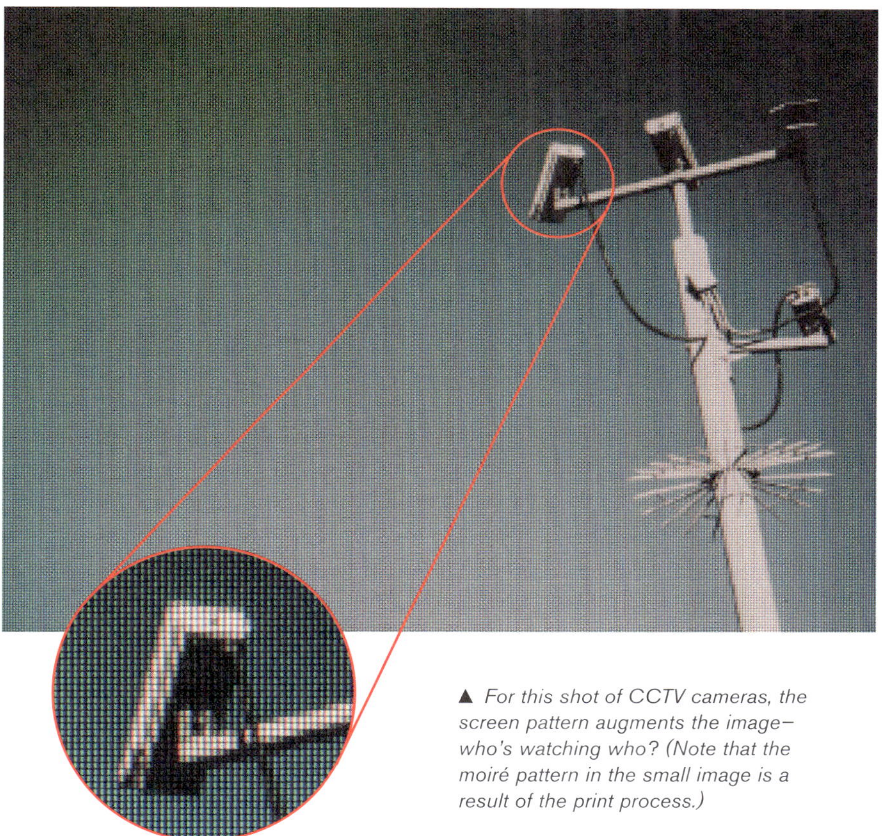

▲ *For this shot of CCTV cameras, the screen pattern augments the image— who's watching who? (Note that the moiré pattern in the small image is a result of the print process.)*

A few words of caution:

- You need to watch out for the "moiré" effect if you're using a digital camera. This effect occurs when the dots/pixels of the screen image "clash" with the grid-like structure of the camera's sensor, resulting in unusual patterns and colors. You can usually avoid this by adjusting the camera position, or by shooting on film instead.

- Shutter speed plays an important part in achieving a clear image: if the exposure time is too short then you can start to see "banding" across the screen (with LCD screens) or a partial image (with CRTs). A very rough rule is to use a shutter speed slower than 1/25 sec., but experiment to see what works best for your setup.

ASSIGNMENT 06

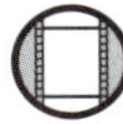
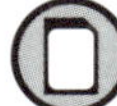
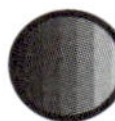
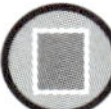

KIT LIST

- Any type of camera (including cameraphone)

TIPS

- If you're really worried about getting it "wrong," shoot two or more images with different framing options to see which one works best.

- Creative crops can be made at the shooting stage or at the processing or printing stage, either by cropping a digital image or negative, or by physically cutting up a print.

SEE ALSO

Off-center subjects create a lot of extra space in the frame, which is ideal if you want to add text or draw or paint onto an image.

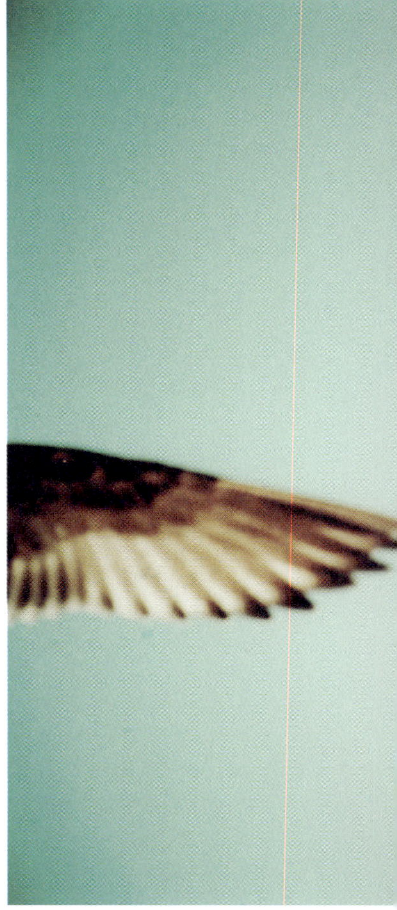

▼ *I was actually trying to get a full-frame shot of a seagull here, but when I did it just looked like... a boring shot of a seagull! This serendipitous shot is way more exciting, precisely because of the cut off, "off-piste" composition that doesn't follow conventional "rules."*

GO OFF-PISTE

The Number One route to a boring composition is to have your subject at the center of the frame. So, mix it up! And that doesn't mean shuffling your subject slightly to one side—take it to extremes! Try putting your subject at the extreme edge of the shot, right up in the corner, or even cut it off with the frame itself. Don't worry about getting it "wrong" or flying in the face of conventional compositional "rules"—those rules aren't mandatory, and sometimes breaking the rules is the route to creativity.

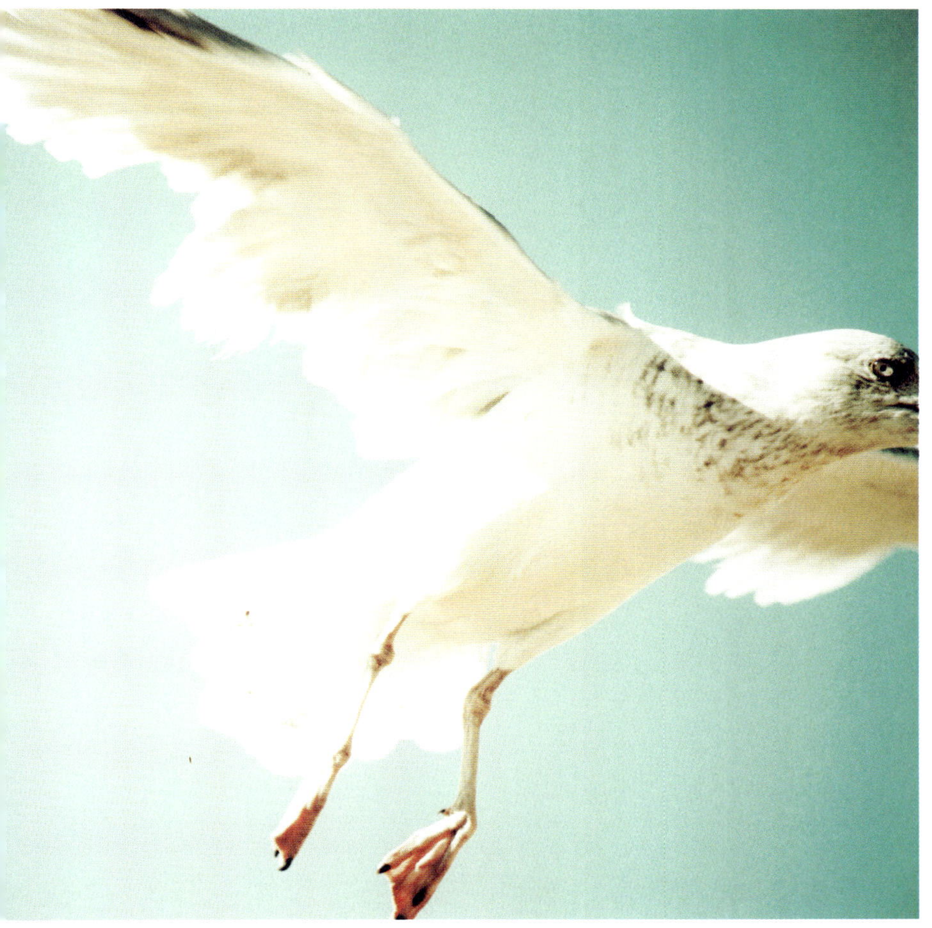

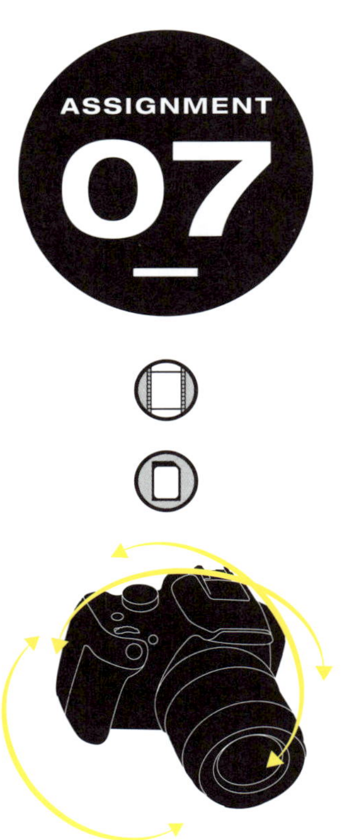

KIT LIST

- Camera with shutter speed control or "night shot" (or similar) mode for long exposures
- Courage!

TIPS

Although you can toss your camera anywhere, the strongest results often come when you shoot in quite dimly lit conditions (indoors or at dusk/night), but with a bright light source close by (a television or neon lights, for example). The dark conditions will naturally encourage longer exposure times, while the bright light(s) will create strong, contrasting patterns and colors in your shot.

SEE ALSO

There are lots of ways to "force" movement into a shot, including shooting from a moving vehicle (Assignment 03), panning the camera (Assignment 09), and zoom bursts (Assignment 13)—each one is different.

CAMERA TOSSING

OK . . . so this experiment needs to start with a safety warning: if you get this one wrong, you might end up trashing your camera. So weigh up the risks—or find an old camera—before you decide to give it a go.

With that out of the way, welcome to the anarchic, abstract world of camera tossing. As the name suggests, the aim of the game is to toss your camera into the air while the exposure is being made, resulting in unpredictable, one-of-a-kind photographs. It really is that simple.

You can toss any camera you like, but to gain a little bit of control (and get instant feedback) a digital camera with shutter speed control (Shutter Priority) or some sort of "night shot" mode and a self-timer is the best place to start. You can pick up some super-cheap point-and-shoot compact cameras on eBay that will work just fine—plus it won't be the end of the world if you drop it.

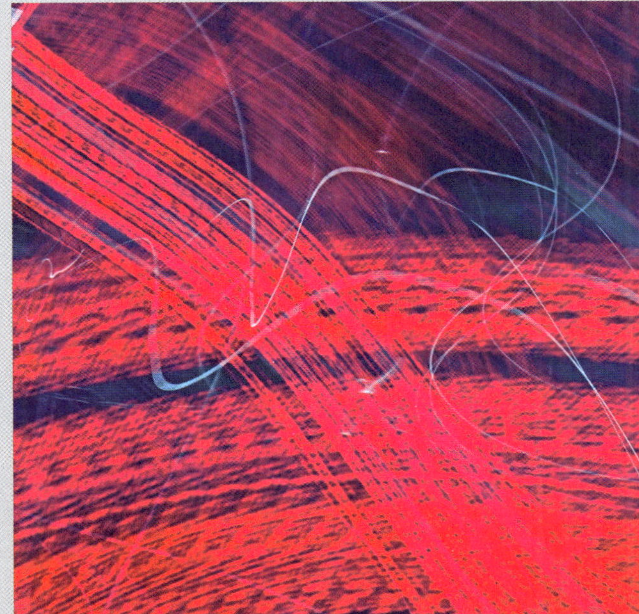

THE PROCESS

1 Set the shutter speed. If you set it too fast, you won't record any blur; too slow and there will be too much blur. A good start point is to set the shutter speed in the region of 1/2–1/8 sec. and experiment from there or use your camera's "night shot" mode.

2 Set the self-timer. If you have the option, set the timer to 1 or 2 seconds; if not, you'll likely have a 10-second countdown.

3 Press the shutter-release to start the timer countdown. Just before you think the camera's going to fire, toss it gently into the air. With luck, you'll have got your timings right and the shutter will open when the camera's airborne, recording a "tossed" image.

4 Catch your camera!

5 Check your shot. If your timing's off or the toss just hasn't worked, adjust the shutter speed (if you need to), reset the self-timer, and have another go. You can also play with the way you toss the camera—adding a gentle spin or throwing it in a looping curve will change the look of your shots.

ASSIGNMENT 08

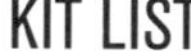

KIT LIST

- Any type of camera (including cameraphone)

TIPS

- Storefronts can offer some surprising juxtapositions that combine reflections off the glass with glimpses of the store's interior.

- Many cities house modern glass- and mirror-fronted office buildings that can be used to create alternative views of iconic monuments.

- Autofocus cameras can struggle to focus accurately when they're aimed at a reflective surface, so be prepared to pick a focus point yourself, or switch to manual focus if that's an option.

REFLECTED REALITY

The world is reflected all around us: in café windows, puddles in the street, automobile paintwork, and pretty much anything else that has a reflective (or semi-reflective) surface. However, unless it's a flat mirror, the image that's being reflected is going to be distorted to a greater or lesser degree. This can make for some great photo opportunities, so next time you're out with your camera, keep your eyes open for these reflected "alternate realities."

▶ *Look for interesting reflections of famous buildings. This is St Paul's Cathedral in London, as seen reflected in the windows of a nearby office block.*

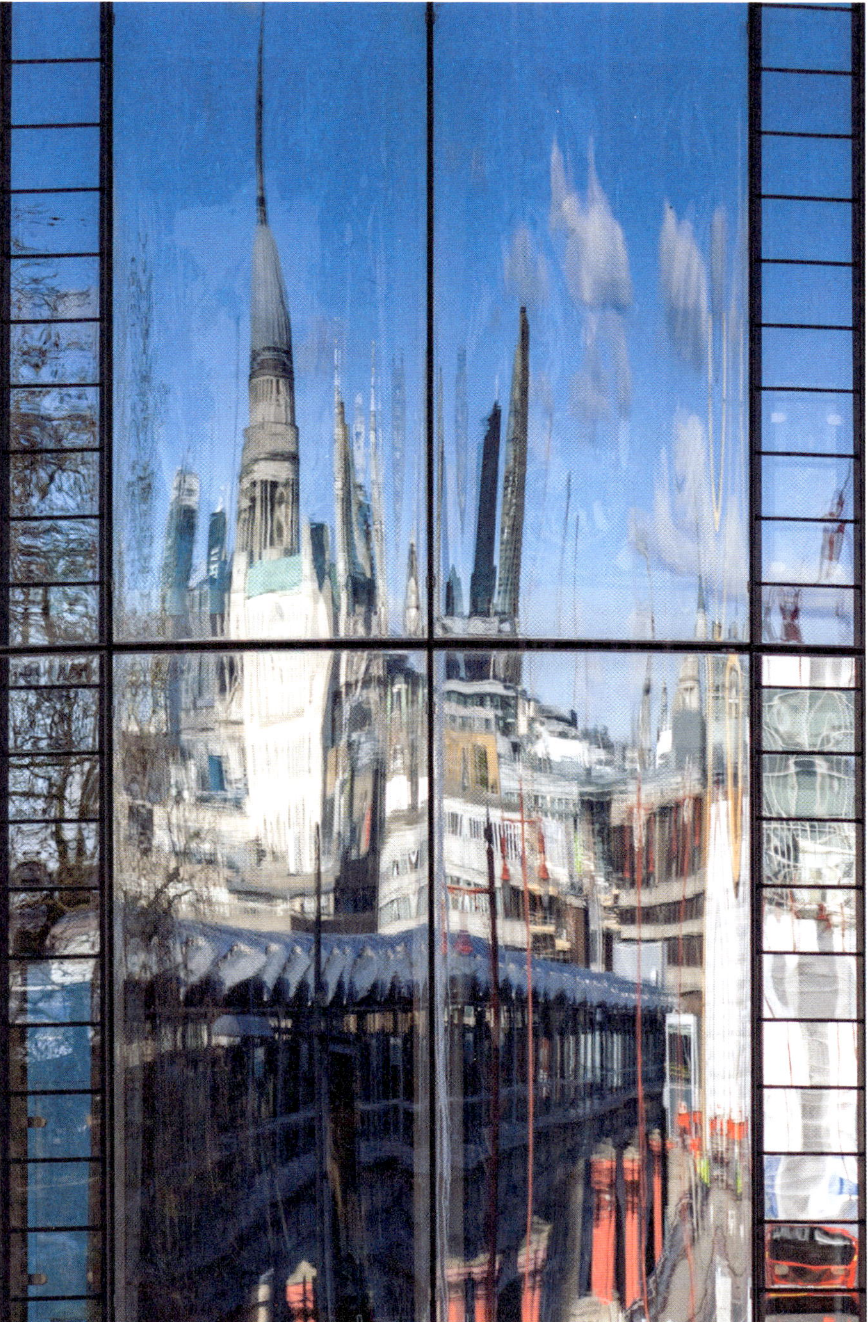

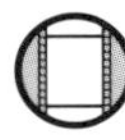

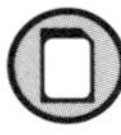

KIT LIST

- Camera with shutter speed control
- Tripod (optional)

TIPS

- You can fake a panned shot using your editing software's Motion Blur filter.

- Following the direction of your subject (upward for vertical subjects such as trees and sideways for subjects that stretch across the frame) emphasizes their natural shape.

- Try combining short pans with multiple exposures (see Assignment 19) to create more Impressionistic images.

SEE ALSO

Shooting from a moving vehicle (Assignment 03), tossing your camera up in the air (Assignment 07), and changing the focal length while you shoot (Assignment 13) are other methods you can use to creatively blur your shots.

PAN-TASTIC

There are plenty of different ways you can inject a sense of dynamism into a static subject by moving your camera, and "panning" your camera is a classic example. Panning simply involves turning the camera sideways, upward, or downward during a long exposure to "smear" the image. Turn the camera to the side to create Impressionistic streaks running across the frame. Pan it up or down to create vertical stripes of color that melt into one another.

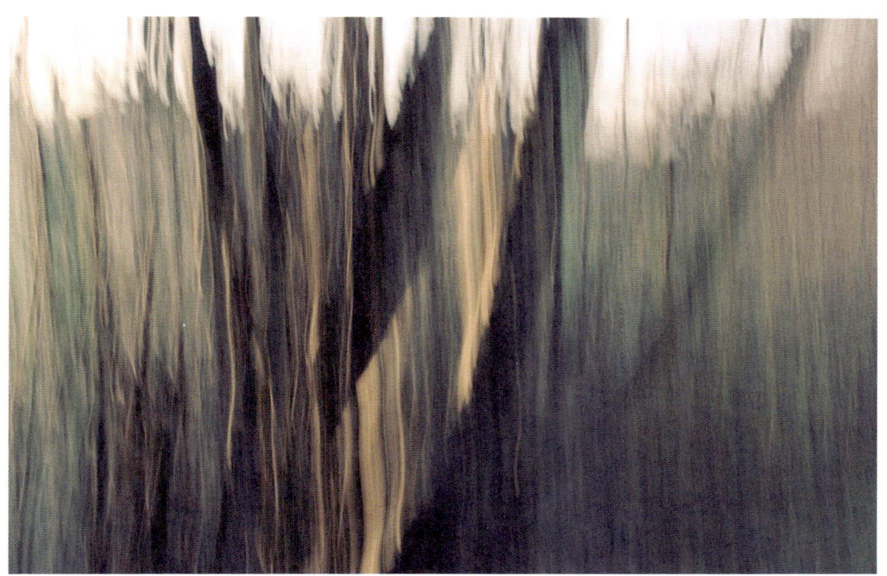

You can handhold your camera, or pan with it mounted on a tripod if you want
more control and a neater, more linear result. Either way, the trick is to set a slow-
ish shutter speed, start moving the camera across your scene, and then fire the
shutter as it moves (rather than shooting first and moving second). The slower the
shutter speed, the more time you will have to pan the camera; and the faster your
movement, the longer the streaks in your image will be. So, experiment with different
combinations of exposure time and panning speed—no two shots will be the same.

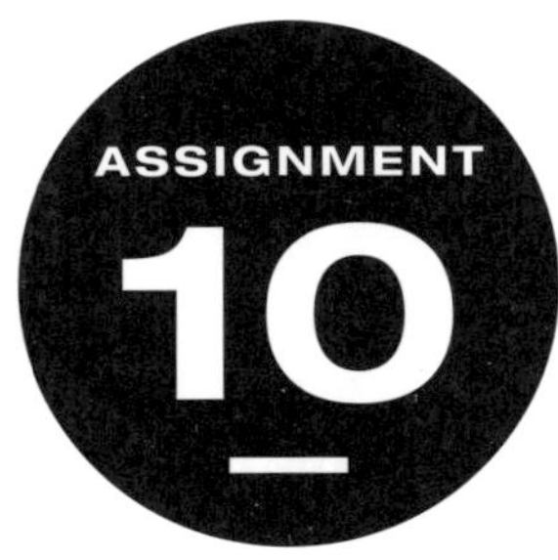

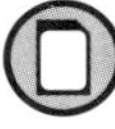

KIT LIST

- Any type of camera (including cameraphone)
- Magnifying glass

TIPS

- "Chromatic aberration" is the technical term for the colored fringes that you might see around the edges of your subject when you photograph through a magnifying glass. Most image-editing software offers some sort of chromatic aberration correction.

- As well as using the magnifying glass parallel to your lens, you can twist and turn it to distort the image.

- Reflections on the glass can be a problem, but a slight adjustment to the camera and magnifying glass angle is usually all you need to do to avoid them.

SEE ALSO

To get even closer with your camera you can convert an empty potato chip can into an extension tube: see Assignment 40 for the "how to."

IT'S A SMALL WORLD

Shooting through a magnifying glass is a low-tech, low-cost macro solution that works with any camera. Sure, you might not get the same tack-sharp results as with a macro lens, and there might be some colored fringing to remove, but don't let that put you off giving the "poor man's" macro lens a go—just hold it in front of your camera lens and shoot what you see!

▶ *For this jewelry shot, I included the magnifying glass as part of the picture, to frame the ring I was photographing.*

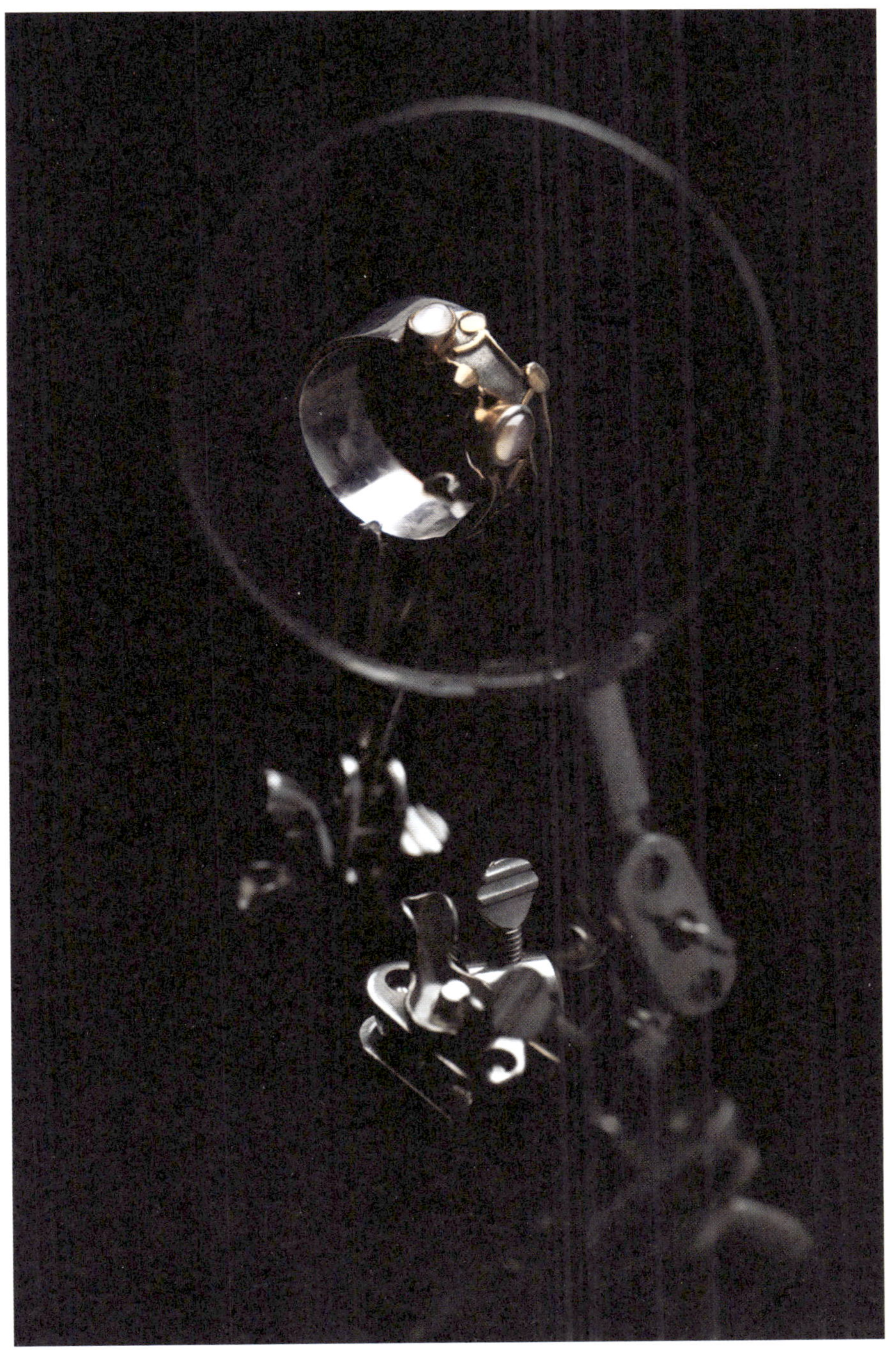

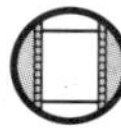

ASSIGNMENT JOURNAL

KIT LIST

- Film camera
- Transparency (slide) film

TIPS

- Slide film uses what is known as an E6 development process, whereas print film uses C41 (worth knowing when you speak to the lab).

- You can also cross-process print film by running it through the E6 (slide film) process, but the results tend not to be as dramatic.

- Experiment with your exposures. Some films respond better to cross-processing if they are overexposed slightly. Do this by manually tweaking the exposure or deliberately setting the film speed on the camera to a lower ISO setting (fooling the camera into giving your shots more light).

- As a last resort, you can "cross-process" your digital images using your editing software, although a lot of so-called cross-processing filters are a pale imitation of the real thing and produce repetitive results.

SEE ALSO

Using colored filters over the lens can transform the look of your cross-processed images, so why not experiment with colored cellophane over the lens (see Assignment 20)?

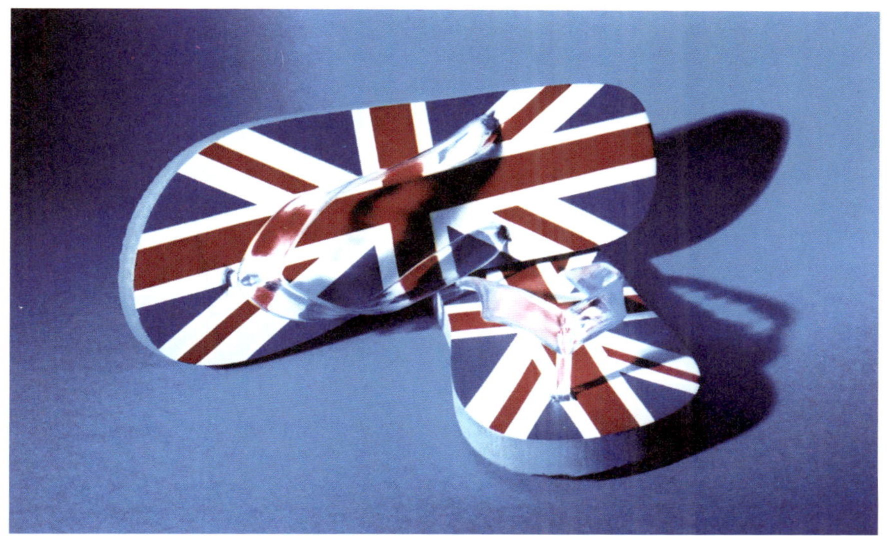
▲ *The "punchy" look of cross-processed film is well-matched to this bright subject.*

CROSS-PROCESSING

Long before computer software let people change the colors of their images at will, creative film photographers experimented with a range of processes that would transform the shots they took. One of the most popular techniques—and one that's still used by some professional photographers because of the unique result it produces—is "cross-processing."

Essentially, all you are doing when you cross-process a film is shooting regular color transparency (or slide) film and then asking your local lab to develop it using the color process designed for print film. It's fairly common, so just ask for your film to be "cross-processed" when you hand it over.

The results you get by processing slide film through the "wrong" chemicals vary from film to film, so you'll need to experiment with different brands to see which ones you like. A "good" film will give you heavily saturated colors and deep blacks, usually with a color shift of some sort (which can be removed if you scan and edit your images). This intensity is the cross-processed look you are after.

KIT LIST

- Digital image
- Editing software

TIP

You can create "analog" repeat patterns by printing your source image out multiple times and physically tiling the prints together. Bear in mind that you'll need an equal number of "straight" prints and "flipped" prints (where the image is reversed), otherwise the pattern isn't going to repeat on itself.

STEP & REPEAT

It's widely accepted in photography and other branches of "art" that patterns can create a sense of harmony in an image. Seeing something repeated over and over again has a similar calming effect to a child hearing a lullaby on a constant loop: it's familiar, consistent, and isn't going to do anything that shocks or scares.

When it comes to photography, patterns are all around us in both the man-made and natural worlds—all you need to do is look for them. However, you can also take things into your own hands and create repeat-pattern images using shots that you've already taken. You can use any image you like, but some of the most effective results come from abstract shots containing obvious geometric elements. Images with diagonal elements can create especially strong repeat patterns, but experiment with a variety of shots to see what works best for you.

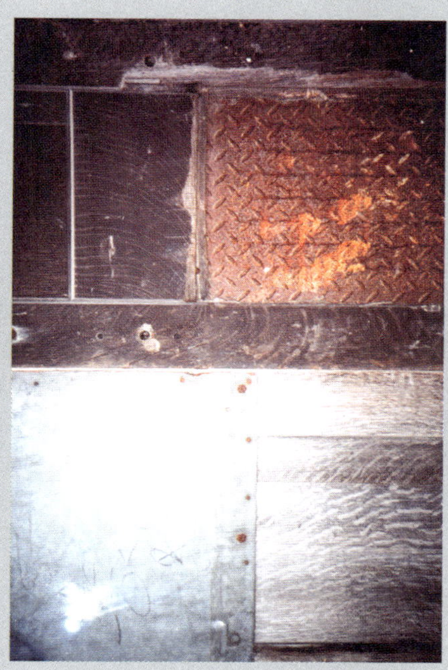

THE PROCESS

1 Open your source image in your editing software. The abstract shot shown here (taken with a point-and-shoot 35mm film compact) is simply a selection of different metal and wood panels that had been used to create a temporary barn door. The shot was scanned and processed to "pop" the color and contrast.

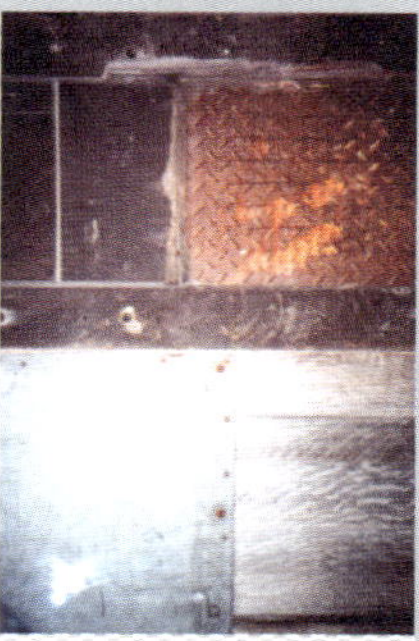

2 Set the "canvas" for your picture larger than the size of the image, so you've got space to repeat it. In Photoshop, use Image > Canvas Size and increase the size of your picture canvas by 200%, both vertically and horizontally. Most image-editing programs will let you do the same thing, but the tool might go under a different name.

3 Duplicate the source image (Layer > Duplicate Layer) and "flip" the new layer horizontally (Edit > Transform > Flip Horizontal). Move your flipped image so it's sitting alongside the original, creating a "mirror image" effect.

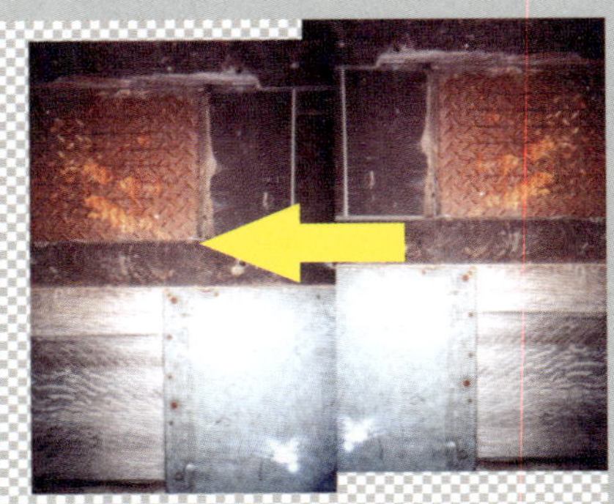

4 Merge the two image layers (Layer > Merge Layers) and then copy the newly merged pair (Layer > Duplicate Layer). This time, flip the new layer vertically (Edit > Transform > Flip Vertical). Then, as in step 3, move the new layer into position so it creates a mirrored repeat pattern.

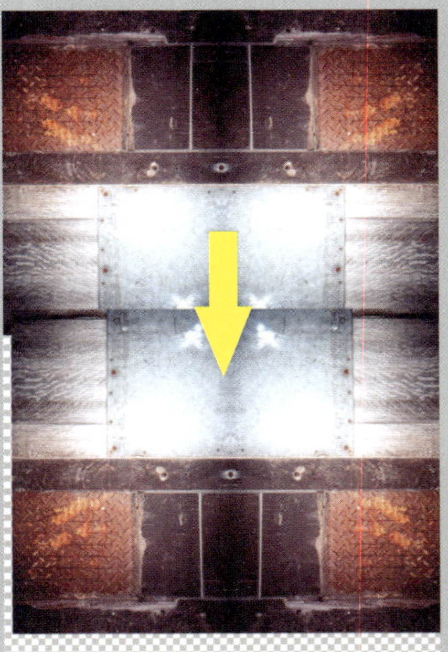

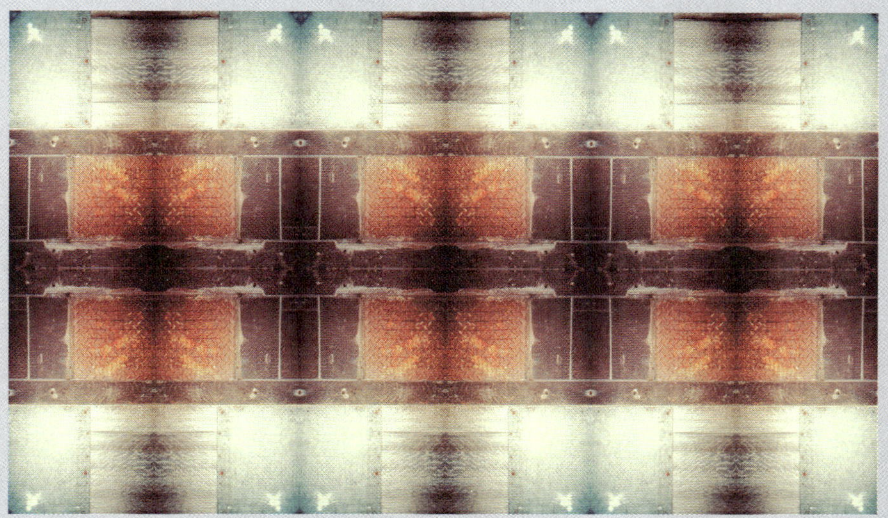

5 You can stop at a four-image repeat (or even a two-image repeat), or you can take things further still. To extend your pattern simply run through steps 2–4 to enlarge the canvas and repeat the image.

For this design, I switched the order of the tiles in step 4 and then repeated the four-shot pattern horizontally (twice) before flattening it down and recoloring it.

ASSIGNMENT JOURNAL

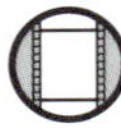

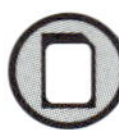

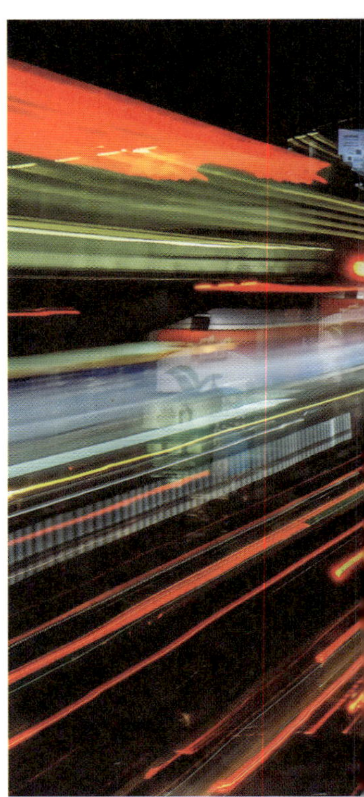

▼ *City lights at night are prime candidates for a zoom burst: this long-exposure shot combines zoom burst elements with traffic trails.*

KIT LIST

- Camera with manually controlled zoom lens (SLR or mirrorless camera)
- Tripod (optional, but recommended)

TIPS

- To totally deconstruct your scene, try combining a zoom burst with panning (Assignment 09), or some other type of camera movement.

- The lines created by a zoom burst will "suck" the viewer into an image, so it's a great way of drawing attention to your subject.

SEE ALSO

If you don't have a camera with a manual zoom lens, shooting from a moving vehicle (Assignment 03), camera tossing (Assignment 07), and panning (Assignment 09) can also be used to "force" movement into a static subject.

ZOOM BURST

We all know that zooming in and out helps us to get that "just about perfect" framing before we fire the shutter, but what about zooming your lens while an exposure is being made? Zoom bursts are all about setting a reasonably slow shutter speed and zooming the lens in or out while a shot is being taken, creating a visual "explosion" in front of the lens. The speed, direction, and how far you zoom—plus the shutter speed you've set—will all affect the result, so experimentation is the key! (A shutter speed in the region of 1/15 sec. is a decent start point.)

Although it looks simple, a successful zoom burst can be quite tricky to achieve, particularly if you're shooting handheld. The problem is, you need a shutter speed that's slow enough to let you zoom, but not so slow that camera shake becomes an issue, and then you also need to perform the actual zooming in (or out) without shaking the camera too much. For this reason, relatively static subjects and a tripod-mounted camera tend to deliver the most successful shots, but don't let that stop you shooting handheld bursts as well!

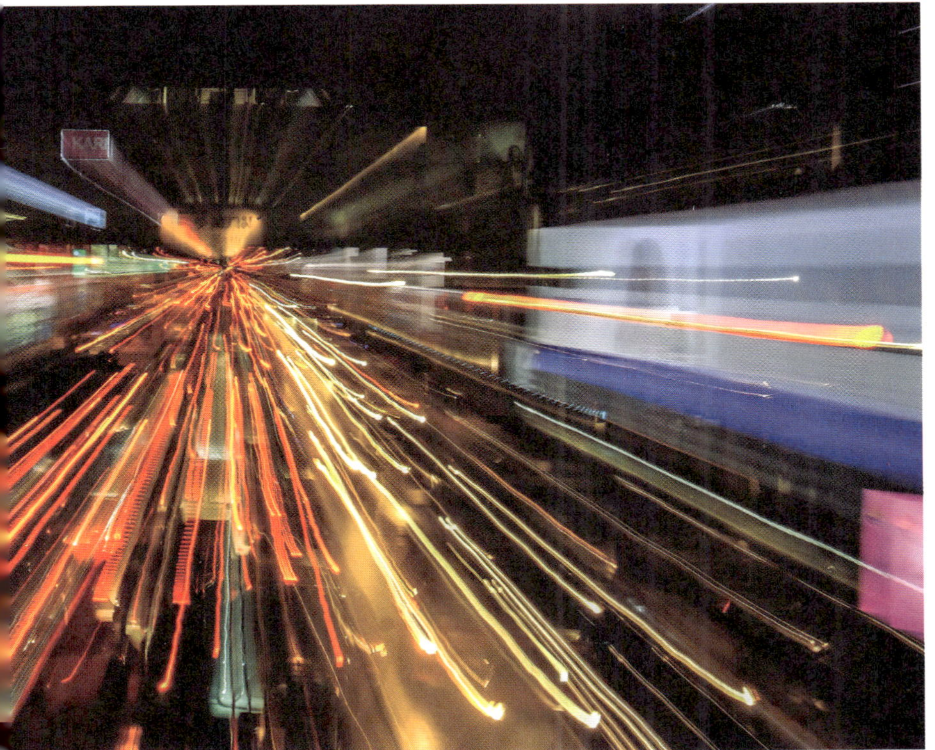

KIT LIST
• Traditional C-type photo print

SEE ALSO
The work of Matthew Brandt is the obvious start point for your investigations, so head over to www.matthewbrandt.com to learn more.

WET PRINTS

In the photographic world, a "wet print" is one that's been made using traditional ("wet") chemical processes, as opposed to prints made using digital printers. However, this experiment takes the notion a step further by emulating the "Lakes and Reservoirs" series by the artist and experimental photographer Matthew Brandt.

For his water-themed series, Brandt visited lakes (and reservoirs) and took two things: photographs of the location—made on color negative film—and some water from it. The photographs were printed as traditional C-type prints, which were then soaked in the water he had collected. Over a period of days, weeks, or even months, the prints remained in soak, which slowly—and naturally—"eroded" the printed image, revealing the colored dye layers that brought the print to life. Using a C-type print and water, you can easily try recreating

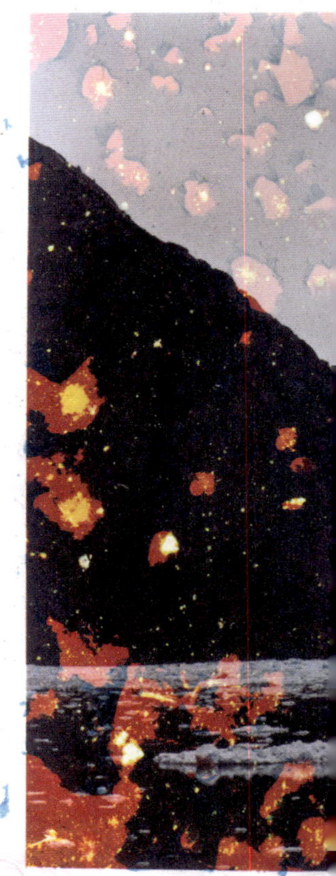

this experiment for yourself. Don't just emulate Brandt, though, see if you can take your wet prints in a different direction. What happens to a reversal (R-type) print, for example? Or a Polaroid print? Or a digital dye-sub print? Or an inkjet print? Do the different types of printing media make a difference?

Alternatively, why not shoot some film and soak that instead of a print? What happens to the emulsion when it's allowed to steep in a water bath for hours, days, or even weeks...?

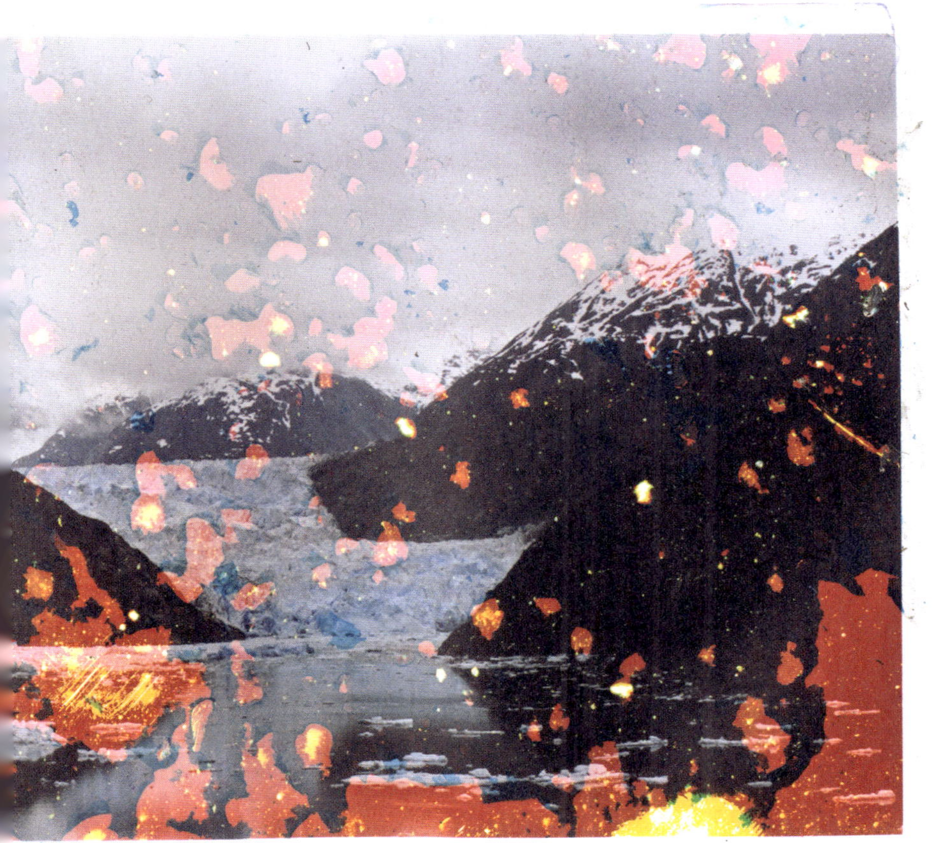

▼ *Patience is a key part of this experiment. After three days soaking outdoors, this print looked exactly the same as it did before it went into the water, but on day four the emulsion had started to peel, contrasting the icy blue glacier in the image with the fiery red/yellow layers of the print.*

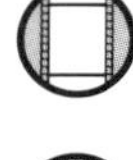

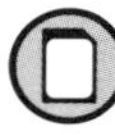

PINHOLE LENS

The theory behind pinhole photography is simple: light passes through a tiny hole and projects an image onto your camera's sensor, film, or even photographic paper. The result is an image with exceptional depth of field (almost everything will be "in focus" because of the tiny aperture), plenty of motion blur (due to exposure times being measured in full seconds or minutes), and a slight overall softness (thanks to the tiny hole and an effect known as "diffraction").

Best of all, a homemade pinhole lens is guaranteed to be a one-off, so you can truly create images that are unique to you. Here's how you make them.

KIT LIST

- Aluminum from empty drinks can
- Modeling clay or eraser
- Ballpoint pen
- Fine sandpaper
- Pin
- Electrical tape
- Camera to mount your pinhole on

SEE ALSO

Pinhole Photography by Eric Renner is the book most traditional pinhole enthusiasts turn to first (especially the second and third editions without "digital" in the title).

TIP

- Using thin brass instead of aluminum will enable you to create a cleaner hole and get (relatively) sharper images.

- Rather than one hole, why not make two (or more) and see what happens when you shoot through a "multi-hole" lens?

- There are countless vintage cameras with broken shutter mechanisms, which are perfect for pinhole conversions—just remove the broken shutter (and the lens) and replace it with a homemade pinhole plate.

THE PROCESS

1 The raw material for your pinhole is the aluminum from an empty drinks can. You don't need much (a 1-inch [2.5cm] square will do) but be careful when cutting it out because this stuff is sharp!

2 Place your pinhole plate on top of a small ball of modeling clay (or an eraser) and use a ballpoint pen to make an indent at the center of the metal.

3 Flip your pinhole plate over, so the indent is forming a peak, and use the fine sandpaper to "thin" the metal.

4 Put the plate back on your modeling clay and gently make a hole using your pin. You want this to be small, so go carefully and take your time—using a "drilling" action is better than pressing hard on the pin.

5 Lightly sand the metal flat where the pin has pushed through it, blow out any dust, and hold your plate up to the light—all going to plan you should have a perfectly round, tiny hole. If not, cut out another plate and start again . . .

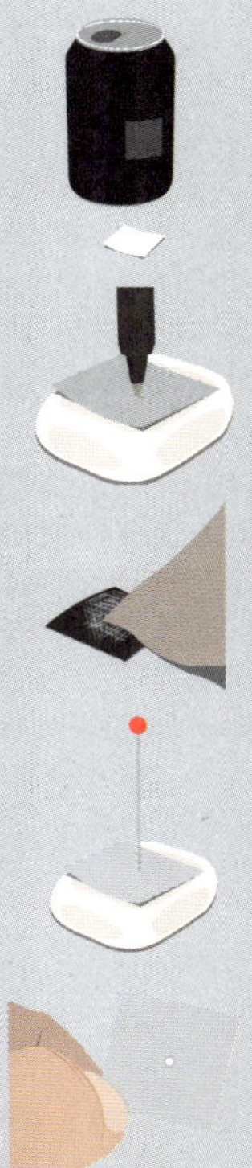

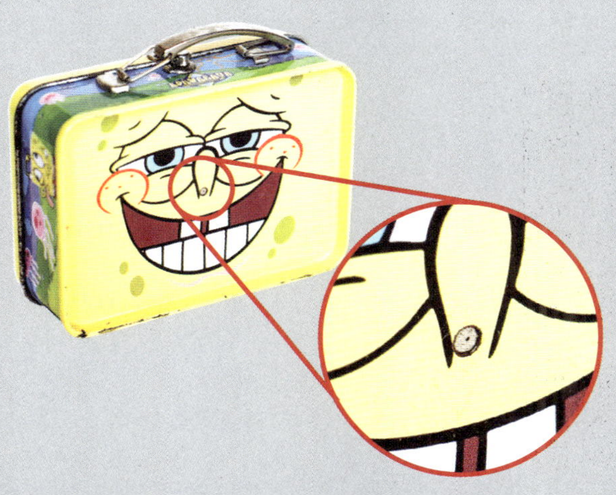

6 Once you've got a "good" hole you need to mount it on something. There are myriad options here, ranging from old cameras to homemade boxes or "found" objects. I mounted this pinhole in a small (3½ x 2½ inch [9 x 6.5cm]) tin which is great for shooting paper negatives on black-and-white printing paper.

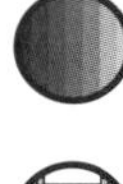

KIT LIST

- Pinhole camera
- Photographic film or paper (depending on camera)
- Lightmeter (handheld or in-camera)
- Exposure table
- Tripod

TIPS

- If you shoot on paper your exposures will be much longer than they would be on film: paper typically has an effective ISO in the region of ISO 3–5!

- When it comes to shooting film in a pinhole camera, negative film is the best option, as it has a much greater tolerance to exposure errors than slide film. In either case, research reciprocity failure as this can affect long exposures (effectively making them longer still).

PINHOLE TAKING

The great thing about pinhole photography is that virtually any light-tight container has the potential to be transformed into a pinhole camera (see Assignment 15). If you are using your own camera it is easiest to make your exposures on single sheets of black-and-white photographic paper, rather than trying to engineer some sort of film-holding and advancing mechanism. This will give you a paper negative that you can contact print to make a positive image or scan and invert (see Assignment 48). But before you can start putting your pinhole lens to use you will need to know its effective aperture, which can be worked out by using the process shown here.

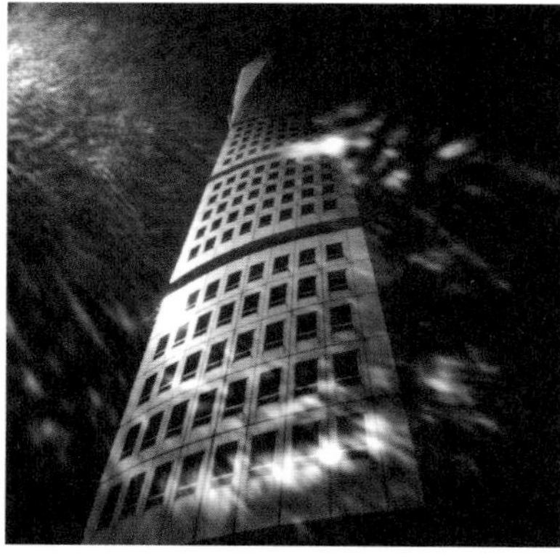

◄ *This photo of Turning Torso, the tallest building in Sweden was taken on traditional photographic film with a pinhole camera.*

THE PROCESS

1   Use a flatbed scanner to scan your pinhole plate, and open it in your image editing software. You can also photograph the plate, but this will not be quite as accurate unless your camera is perfectly square to the plate.

2   Zoom into your scan/photograph and use your image editing software's ruler tool to measure the diameter of the pinhole (right). In this instance the diameter was just under 0.018in (0.45mm).

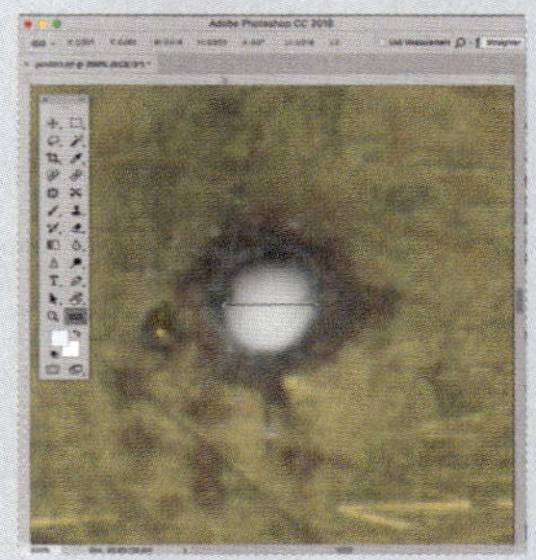

3   To convert the pinhole size into an aperture or "f/stop," you need to know the distance between the pinhole and the film/photo paper in your pinhole camera (the focal length). Divide the focal length by the pinhole diameter and this will give you the working aperture. For example, if your camera has a focal length of 4in (10cm) and your pinhole has a diameter of 0.018in (0.45mm), the aperture is f/222.

4   Go online and search for "pinhole exposure calculator." This will take you to websites where you can generate a custom exposure grid based on your pinhole aperture, as shown below.

▼ *An exposure grid lets you use the exposure meter in a regular camera or a handheld lightmeter to determine your pinhole exposure times. Simply take an exposure reading with your camera (or lightmeter) and cross-reference the aperture/shutter speed with the pinhole aperture. In the grid below—which represents a small part of a much larger grid—an exposure reading of 1/60 sec. at f/8 with a "regular" camera or lightmeter, would translate to a 12 sec. exposure with an f/222 pinhole (the ISO is set based on the film/paper you are using in your pinhole camera).*

f/8	f/16	f/222
1/1000 SEC.	1/250 SEC.	1 SEC.
1/500 SEC.	1/125 SEC.	2 SEC.
1/250 SEC.	1/60 SEC.	3 SEC.
1/125 SEC.	1/30 SEC.	6 SEC.
1/60 SEC.	1/15 SEC.	12 SEC.
1/30 SEC.	1/8 SEC.	24 SEC.
1/15 SEC.	1/4 SEC.	49 SEC.

ASSIGNMENT

17

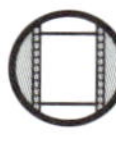

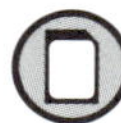

KIT LIST

- Camera with aperture control
- Black card
- Craft knife/scissors

TIPS

- Out-of-focus "point light sources" such as Christmas tree lights or "fairy" lights create strong bokeh shapes. The more obvious the lights, the more obvious the bokeh.

- The shape of your filter will be most apparent when you shoot with a wide aperture setting. For this reason, an SLR or mirrorless camera with a fast prime lens works best (a lens with a maximum aperture in the region of f/1.8 is ideal).

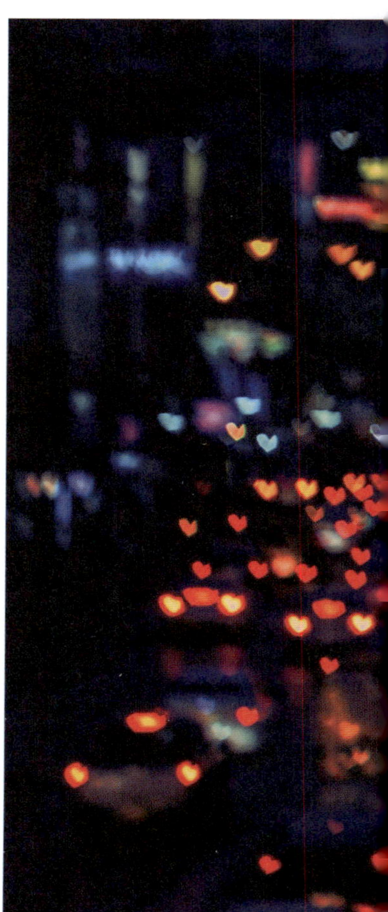

▼ *Bokeh filters work best when there are distinct "point light sources" that are out of focus—like these car and street lights at night.*

BOKEH FILTERS

The word "bokeh" is commonly used to refer to the appearance of out-of-focus points in an image—the softer, smoother, and rounder these defocused points appear, the "better" the bokeh is said to be. However, you can also have fun with the bokeh in your images by creating shapes from the out-of-focus points using homemade filters.

To create your own bokeh shapes, cut a disc of card that will fit over the front of your lens. At the center of the card, cut out your bokeh shape—a star, a heart, a crescent, whatever (solid shapes that are easy to "read" work best). Fit your card bokeh filter over your camera's lens, set the widest aperture, and shoot. Any obvious out-of-focus highlights will now take on the shape of your bokeh filter.

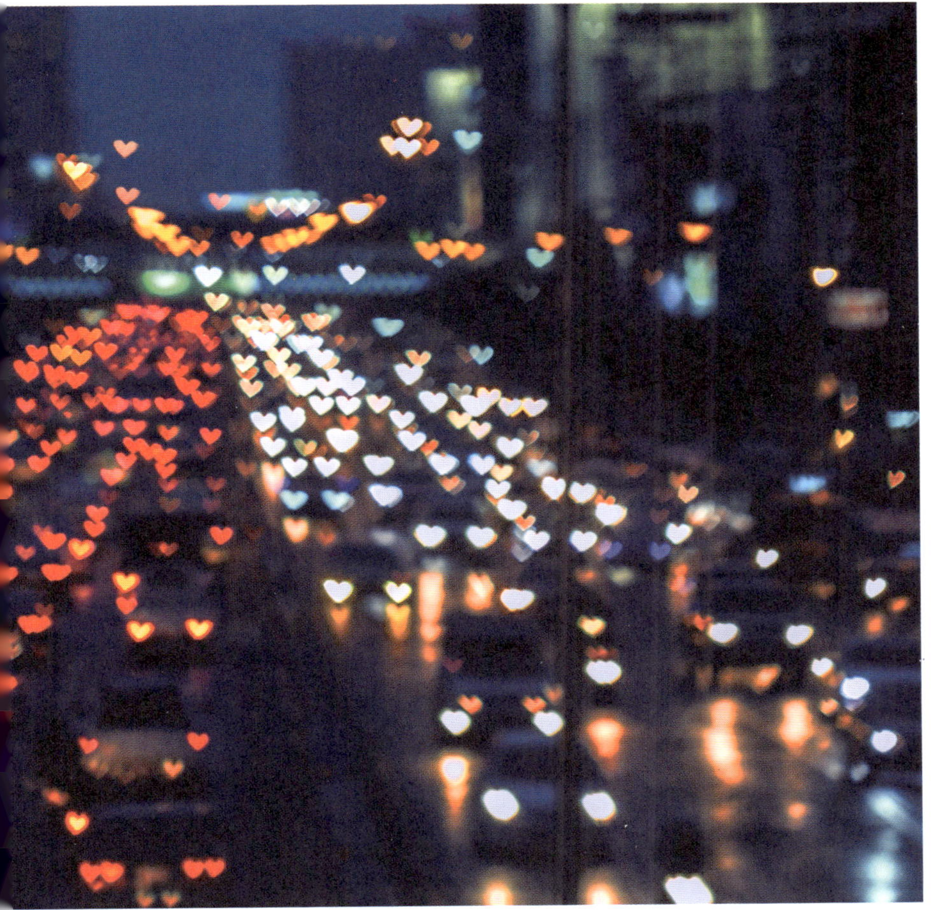

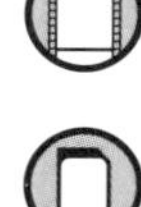

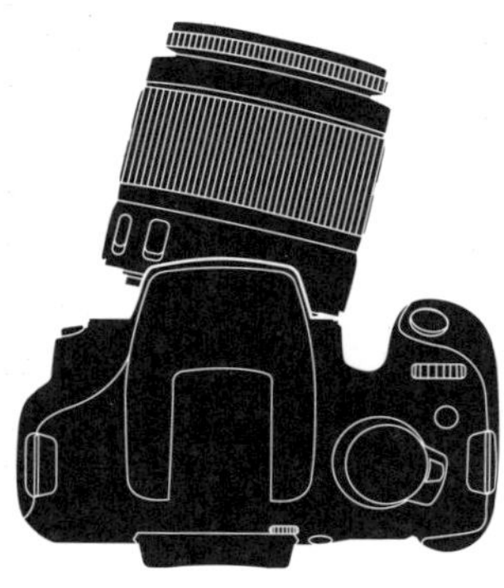

KIT LIST

- Interchangeable lens camera
- Lens (see Tips for more details)

TIPS

- As a rough guide, a standard prime lens designed for a camera system "one size up" from the camera you're using is the ideal option: use a full-frame 50mm prime lens on a compact mirrorless camera or APS-format DSLR, or a medium-format lens in the region of 80mm if you're using a 35mm SLR or full-frame DSLR.

- Because you aren't attaching the lens to the camera, the lens mount is less relevant: there are plenty of old manual prime lenses on eBay to choose from.

- Hardcore freelensers will sometimes remove the rear mount and aperture control from a lens to get it closer to the sensor for more "extreme" results (just be very careful that the back of the lens doesn't damage the mirror in the camera).

SEE ALSO

You can also shift the focus in your images by making your own tilt lens adaptor, as outlined in Assignment 39.

FREELENSING

Freelensing is a low-cost, low-tech way of (roughly) emulating the effect you can get by shooting with a tilt-shift lens or large-format camera, where you can turn the lens to the side or up/down to adjust the plane of focus. The trick is really quite simple: you take an interchangeable lens camera and a lens, but you don't mount the lens. Instead, you hold it in front of the lens mount so you're free to move it around. Tilting and turning the lens will let you alter the plane of focus to get some great shallow-focus shots.

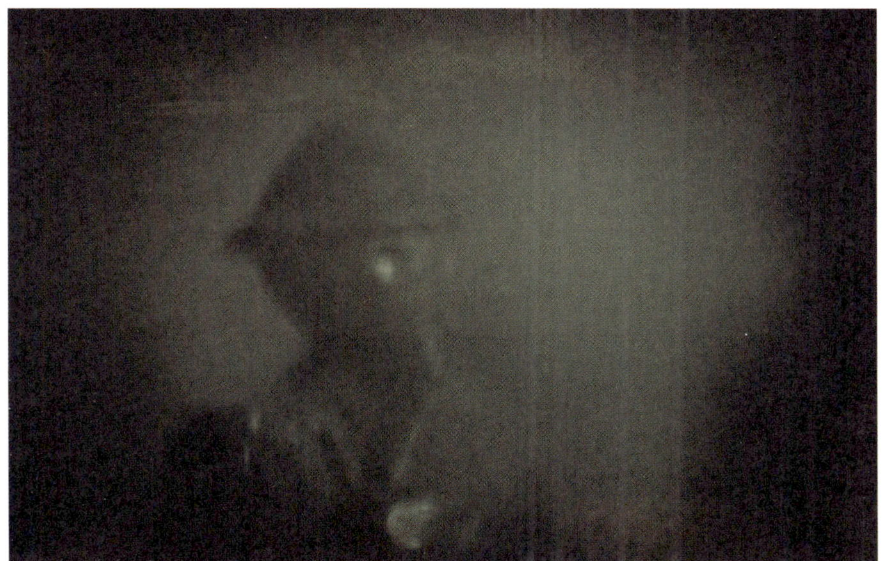

WARNING!

Freelensing isn't dangerous, but you need to be a little more careful than usual when your camera lens isn't attached—you don't want to drop or damage either one through not paying sufficient attention.

A major downside to freelensing is dust. Because you're using your camera without a lens attached, dust will find its way onto your sensor, so it's a good idea to familiarize yourself with how to clean the sensor.

▲ *Freelensing can easily create images that are suggestive rather than sharp. In this photograph of a vintage toy soldier, the freelensing haze and noxious processing both add to the claustrophobic atmosphere of the image.*

Obviously, working like this has multiple drawbacks. Focusing is *waaaaaay* harder than normal, and you'll have to work out your exposures manually, but that's all part of the freelensing challenge. Stick with it and your patience will pay off—you will be rewarded with some unique shots.

KIT LIST

- Camera (your choice of camera dictates how easy or how difficult this is)
- Tripod (optional)

TIPS

- To shoot multiple exposures on a manual 35mm film camera, you will need to hold the camera's "rewind" button while you wind the film on. This will cock the shutter, ready for the next shot, but prevent the film from moving.

- Working out the exposure settings on film for a multiple exposure shot isn't easy, but as a start point you should underexpose each shot by 1 stop if you're combining two frames to end up with the "right" exposure overall.

- A great way of adding an element of serendipity to your multiple exposures is to "double-shoot" a roll of 35mm film—or shoot with the same film twice. Load and shoot the roll the first time, underexposing it by 1 stop, and then reload the film into the camera the next time you go out and shoot it again, also underexposing by 1 stop.

MULTIPLE EXPOSURES

Multiple exposures are all about combining more than one shot in a single frame. There are countless options here: you can add texture to images (you could shoot a portrait, then the sidewalk to add the granular asphalt texture, for example); you can combine disparate elements in a single image to create pre-Photoshop-style visual effects; or you can simply handhold the camera and shoot the same subject repeatedly on the same frame to create an impressionistic result (as shown opposite).

How easy the process is will depend on the camera you're using. Some digital cameras have multiple exposure options built in that automate the process, making it as easy as point-and-shoot photography, while manual 35mm SLRs require a little more effort when it comes to setting the exposure and loading your film (see Tips).

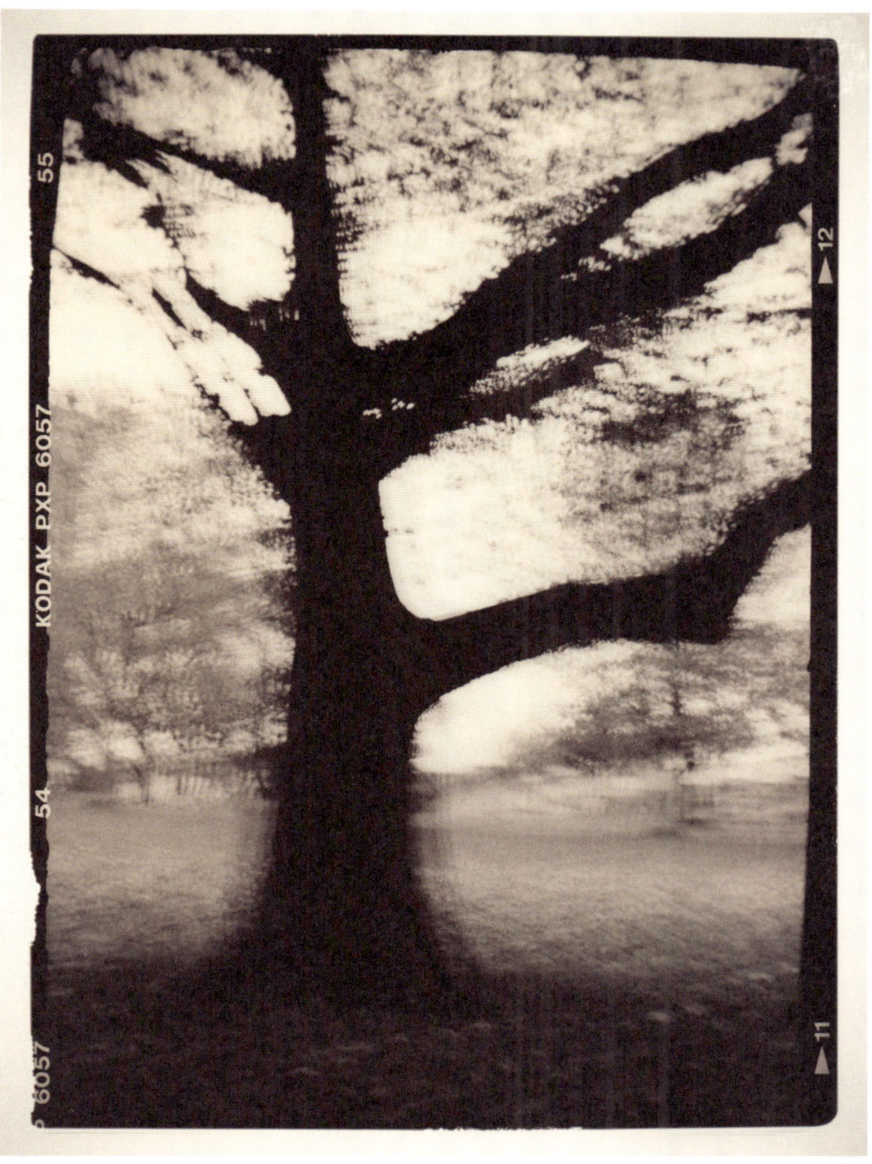

▲ *This multiple exposure was taken using a vintage box camera. I simply handheld the camera and took five or six shots in rapid succession, without winding the film on.*

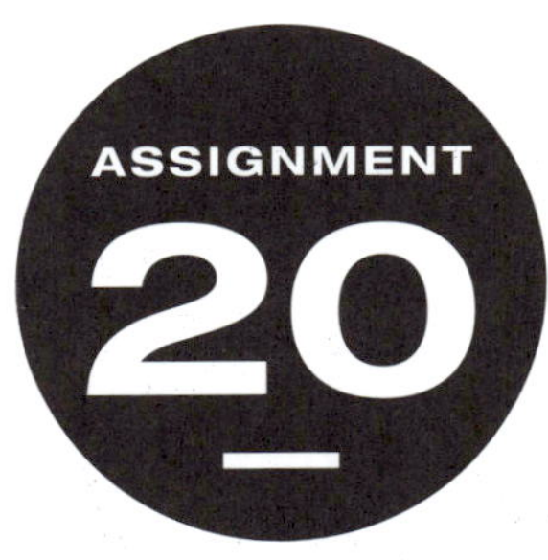

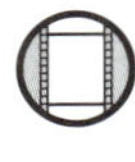

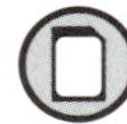

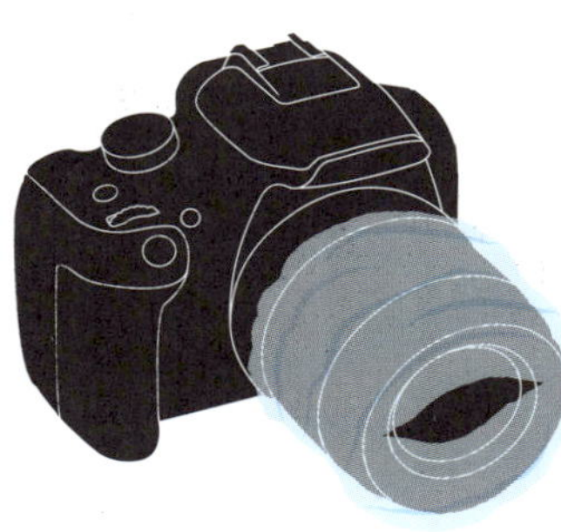

TIPS

- As well as plastic wrap, experiment with vacuum-formed, clear-plastic packaging—the more irregular the shape, the better.

- Try colored materials as well as clear: colored candy wrappers can be used to tint and tone some or all of a shot, for example.

- If your camera is struggling to focus (and you have the choice), switch to manual focus instead of autofocus.

◀ *Covering part of your lens with plastic wrap and leaving some of it clear will determine which areas are and aren't sharp.*

▶ *Experiment with other types of clear plastic. Shooting through the packaging of a child's toy doll has created a distinct "spot" of focus in this shot.*

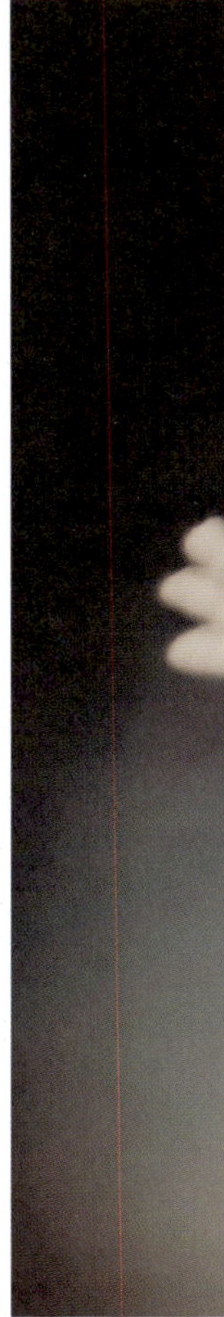

KIT LIST

- Any type of camera (including cameraphone)
- Plastic wrap (or similar)

SEE ALSO

Shooting through frosted (or wet) glass can also transform what your camera sees—head to Assignment 37 for details.

PLASTIC FANTASTIC!

Find yourself some plastic wrap and use it to cover—or partly cover—your lens while you shoot. The result? Parts of the image can be sharply focused, while other areas are reduced to a beautiful blur. You can use any camera you like for this experiment, and even shoot with it set to full Auto rather than messing around with the settings. This is all about playing with the direction, thickness, and even type of plastic you use.

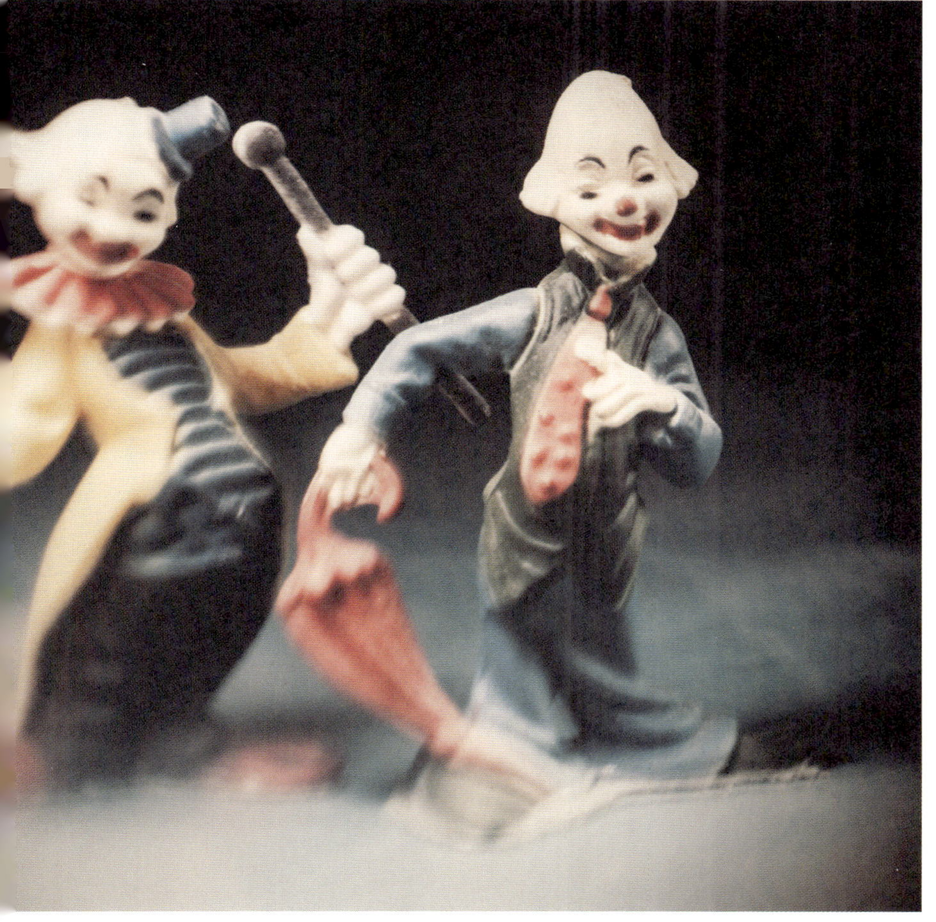

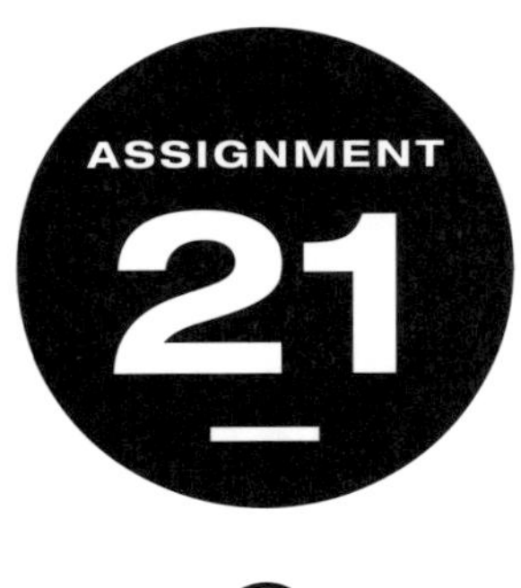

REDSCALE

Like cross-processing (see Assignment 11), redscale is an experimental process with film at its heart. Essentially, all you're going to do here is load your film "back to front," so the emulsion is facing away from the lens, rather than toward it. When you do this, light passes through the backing layer and the red-sensitive layer of the film first, so your images will experience some often-radical color shifts (typically red-yellow, hence "redscale"). How extreme these color shifts are will depend on the film you use, so part of the experiment should be to find an emulsion you like.

When it comes to choosing your film to start with, you've got two options. The simplest is to buy redscale film, which is already emulsion-side-out, so you can just load it up and shoot as normal. Alternatively, if you're shooting with 35mm, you can "roll your own" redscale. This takes a bit more effort, but it'll cost less and—more importantly—the results will be more interesting and unique.

KIT LIST

- Film camera
- Redscale film
  OR
- Film camera
- Regular color negative film
- Scissors
- Sticky tape
- Darkroom/changing bag/blacked-out room

SEE ALSO

If you like to push your film in new directions, why not try cross-processing it (see Assignment 11)?

TIP

- If you're rolling your own film you'll likely need to increase the exposure because the light has to pass through the film's backing layer—overexposing by 1–2 stops should be enough, but it's worth bracketing your exposures until you know how your film reacts.

- You can shoot medium-format redscale, but the backing paper on 120 film makes it much harder to roll your own. It's far easier to buy ready-rolled film or use 220 film instead (if your camera will let you).

- When you take your film to be processed, be sure to tell the lab what you've done—otherwise they might think something's gone wrong and try to correct the colors.

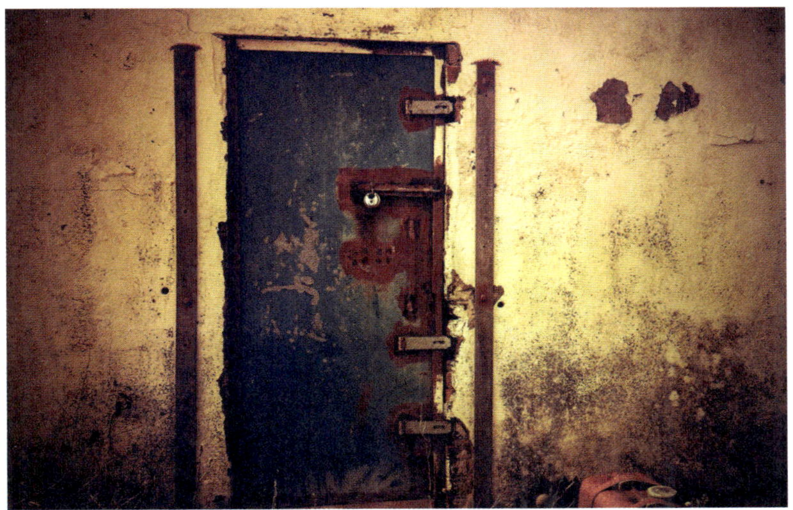

▲ *Redscale gets its distinctive look because the film's blue-sensitive layer is exposed last (rather than first), meaning it has less effect on the image.*

THE PROCESS

1   Cut the end of your film square, to lose the "leader." Then, in TOTAL DARKNESS—in a darkroom, changing bag, or blacked-out room—pull the film carefully out of the cassette. Cut the film off, so there's an inch or two protruding from the cassette.

2   Turn the film (or cassette) round so the emulsion side of the cut-off film is lined up with the NON-emulsion side of the film protruding from the cassette. Tape the two together.

3   Still in TOTAL DARKNESS, wind the film carefully back into the cassette. Make sure you don't wind it all the way, though—you need to cut yourself a new leader. You can now load and shoot the film like any other.

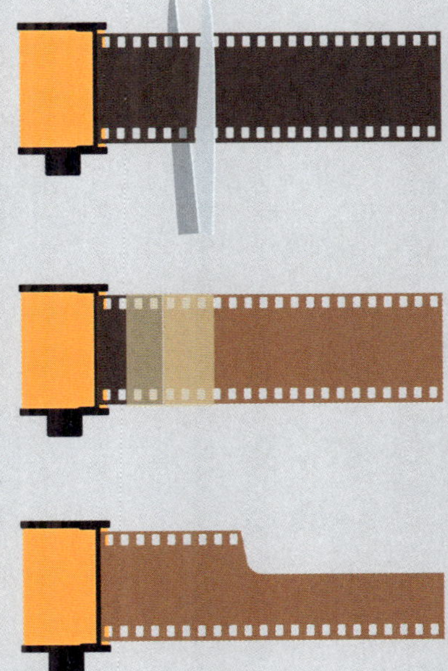

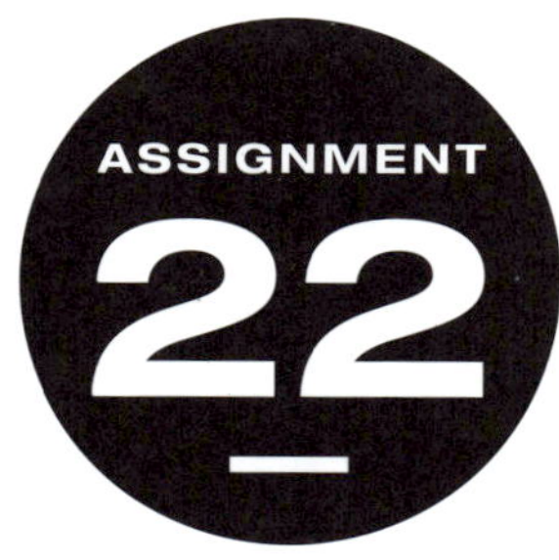

ASSIGNMENT 22

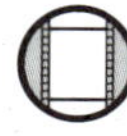
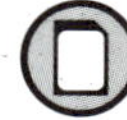
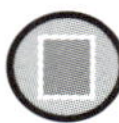

KIT LIST
• Any type of camera (including cameraphone)

TIPS
• If you're working digitally you could give your shots Polaroid-esque borders for a more authentic Hockney vibe.

• Moving position with your camera between individual frames will exaggerate the disparity between the shots—you could even photograph "around" a subject.

SEE ALSO
• David Hockney is the "granddaddy" of this type of image, so your research should start with him.

• Hockney's technique also covered less structured joiners, as you will see in Assignment 23.

▼ *This shot of a toy car was taken using a macro lens and extension tubes on a digital SLR. The individual frames were then processed for "punch" and given a Polaroid-style border before being assembled into a joiner.*

JOINERS #1

David Hockney, the British "Pop" artist, often used instant Polaroid to create large-scale photo-collages. These "joiners" were made up of multiple shots of the same subject, usually taken—handheld—from subtly different positions. The prints were then assembled to create a grid-like image with a distinctly Cubist feel.

A "Hockney joiner" can feature any subject and use any camera you like. You can print your images out and assemble them to create your patchwork grid, piece them together in your editing software, or shoot using instant film for the authentic Hockney look. The key is to shoot handheld and not to worry about images overlapping (or gaps appearing)—having slightly different viewpoints adds to the look of the final image.

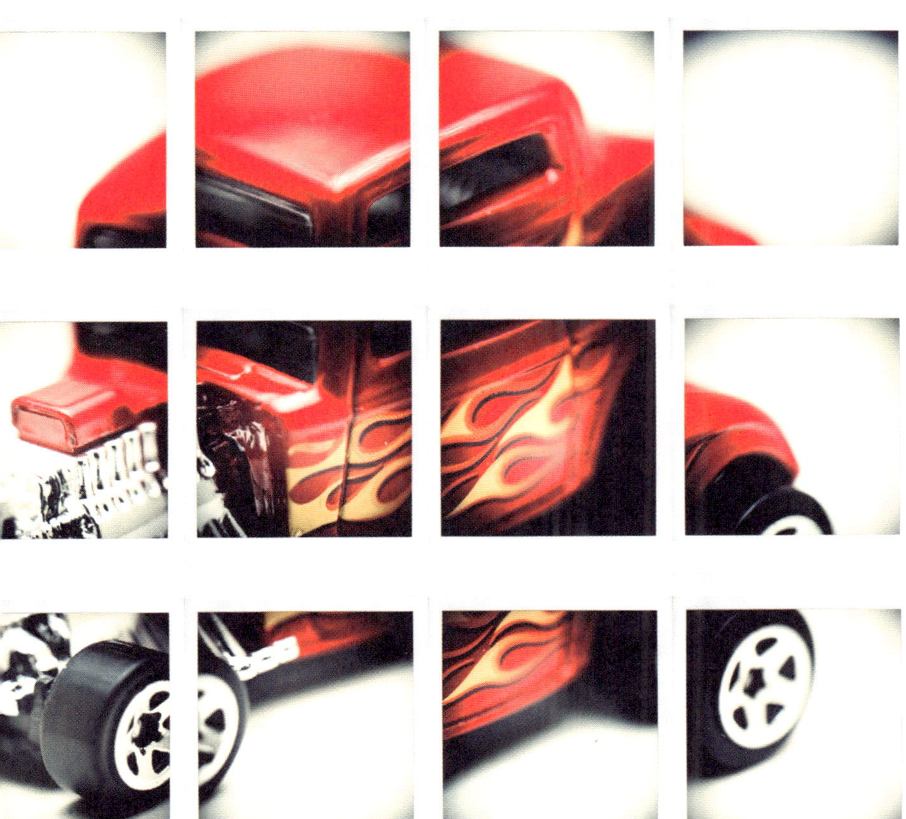

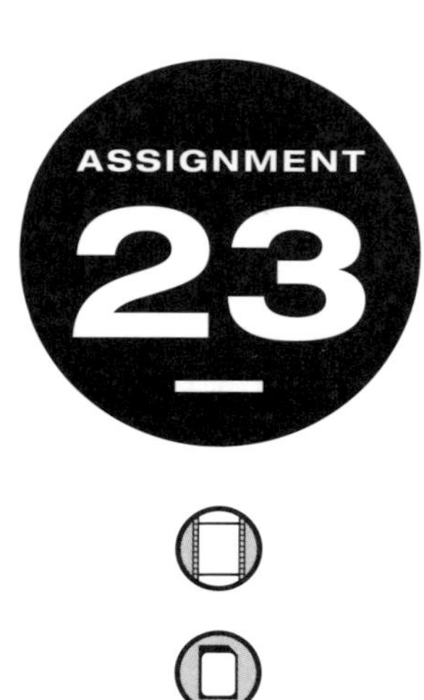

KIT LIST

• Prints or digital images

TIP

You don't necessarily need to take a lot of shots to create this type of image. Instead, handhold your camera and shoot the "big picture" that you want as your end result multiple times. Deliberately change the camera position, exposure, and/or focus with each shot and make a large print of each frame. Cut or tear these prints to make many smaller pieces to reassemble.

SEE ALSO

• As the "creator" of this technique, your research should start with David Hockney.

• To play with Hockney's structured joiners, turn to Assignment 22.

JOINERS #2

As well as his rigid grids of Polaroids (see Assignment 22), David Hockney also took a more fluid approach to his joiner images. Sometimes this meant taking 100s of shots with a 110-format camera and assembling the prints to create a "seamless" image that still revealed subtle differences, thanks to changes in the handheld viewpoint and the time taken between the exposures. You can take this a step further, though, by deliberately messing with the exposure and focus between shots: shoot some darker, some lighter, some in focus, some out, and then assemble the results to build your grid-less joiner.

▶ *You don't necessarily have to use the same subject for your joiners. Maybe you could create a single portrait from different family members, or a landscape using elements from different locations. Mix it up and see what happens.*

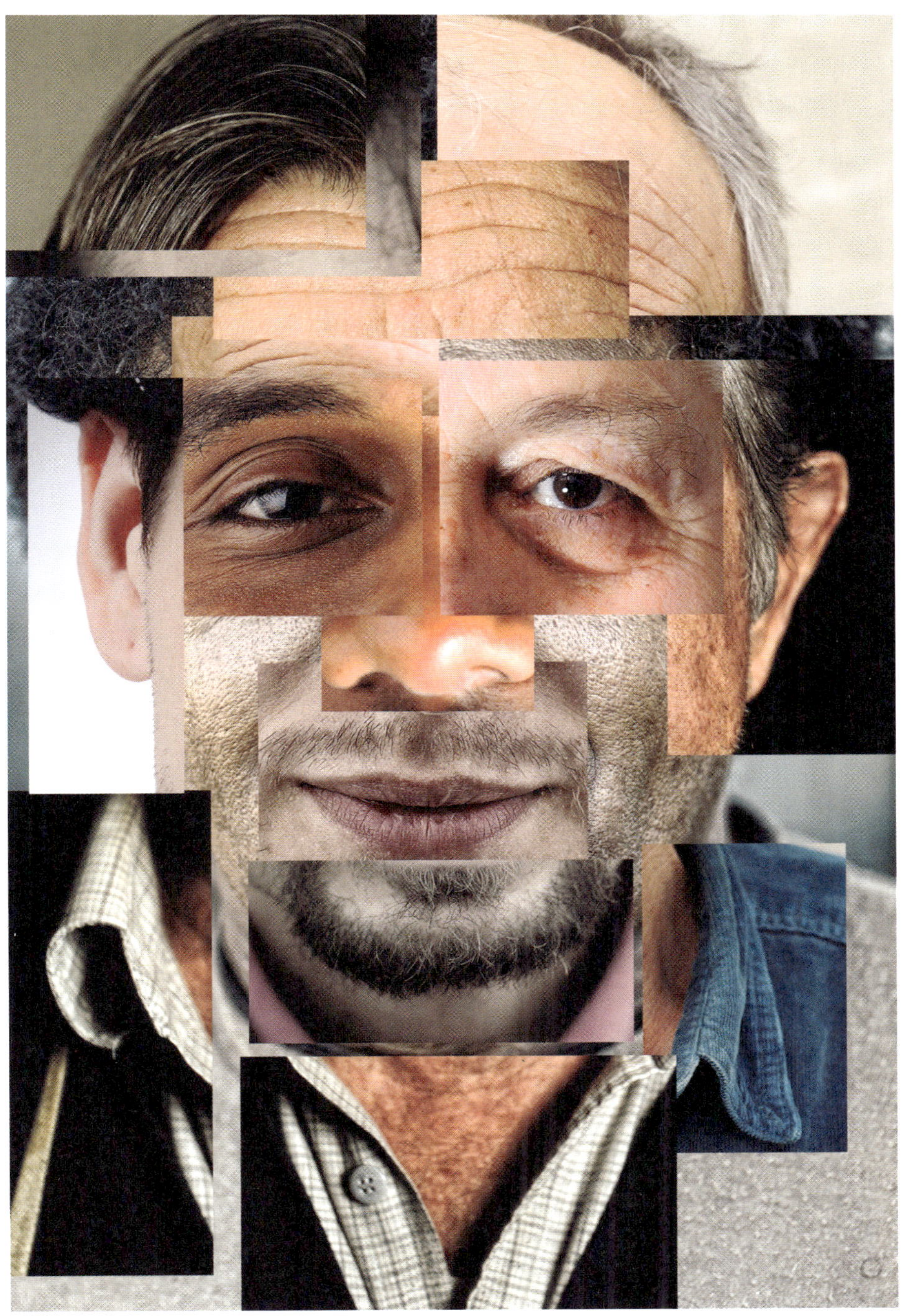

KIT LIST

• Flatbed scanner

TIPS

• A scanner has an incredibly shallow depth of field and the light it produces will "fall off" (darken) quite quickly. The means that anything on the glass platen will be sharply focused and well lit, but anything slightly away from the glass will be thrown out of focus.

• You don't need to use the latest scanner model for your experiments: older scanners are just as capable when it comes to creating high-resolution images (and at a fraction of the cost).

▶ *Flowers make great "scanography" subjects: most of the time the scanner's lid will act like a flower press, gently squashing them against the glass platen so they're sharply focused. Having scanned these flowers I processed them and added a paper border.*

SCANNER ART

There was a time when pretty much every photographer had a scanner to bring all their prints (and film) into the digital age. Today that job has almost inevitably been done, though, so a used scanner can be picked up for next-to-nothing online or in yard sales. That makes them the perfect start point for this experiment, which uses a scanner as a camera.

Simply place your subject on the scanner's glass platen and scan it as if it were a photographic print or document—it's that easy. For your experiments you can try making photograms, creating photo-realistic images of found objects, or producing abstract pieces. It all depends on what you choose to scan and how.

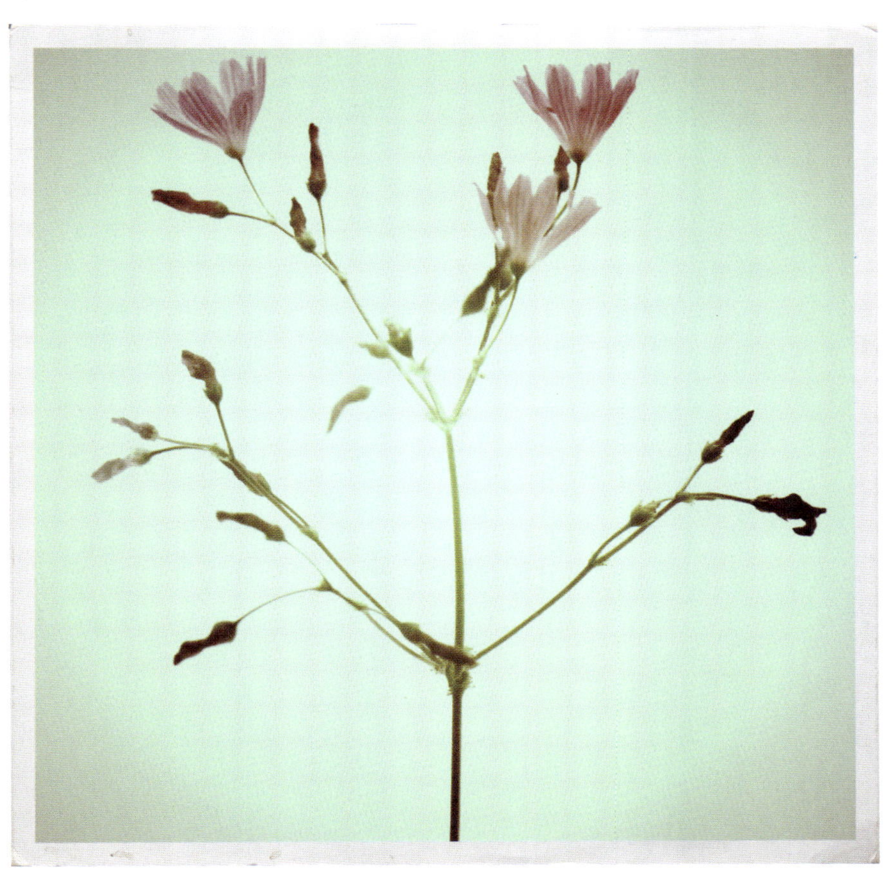

ASSIGNMENT JOURNAL

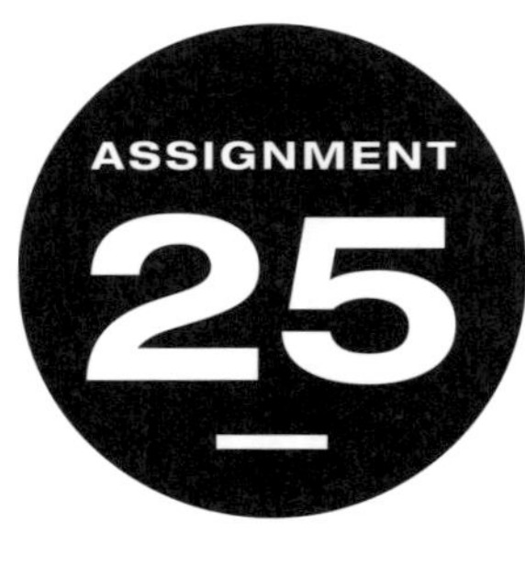

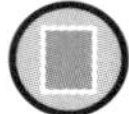

KIT LIST

- Photo print
- Copier

TIPS

- This experiment can be hard to do in a copy shop, unless they're going to let you take control of the copier. A better option is a copier that you can access in your office, school, or local library (especially if you don't have to pay for the copies).

- Color copiers and black-and-white or mono copiers degrade the image in different ways. As a rule, mono copiers tend to give the "grittiest" results as the tonal range gets reduced to blocks of black and white.

- Play around with the copier's brightness and scaling options.

SEE ALSO

You can use your copy art images as the start point for multiple alternative techniques: they lend themselves well to overpainting, staining, and toning (see Assignments 28, 35, and 49).

COPY ART

Essentially, all you do, is make a copy of a photo print, and then take that copy and copy it again. In fact, you can make as many copies as you like. Watch what happens as the tonal range and detail in your original print are slowly eroded with each copy. When you get the "decisive" degraded image, stop.

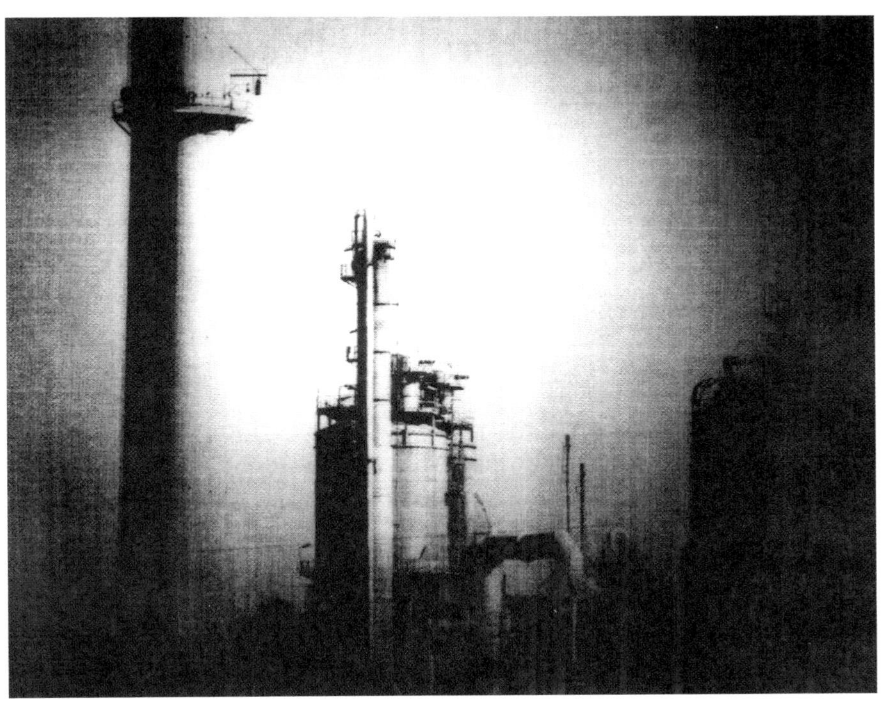

▲ *It only took a few color copies of a black-and-white photo of a power station to create this image, complete with an unexpected color "pop" at the top left.*

ASSIGNMENT JOURNAL

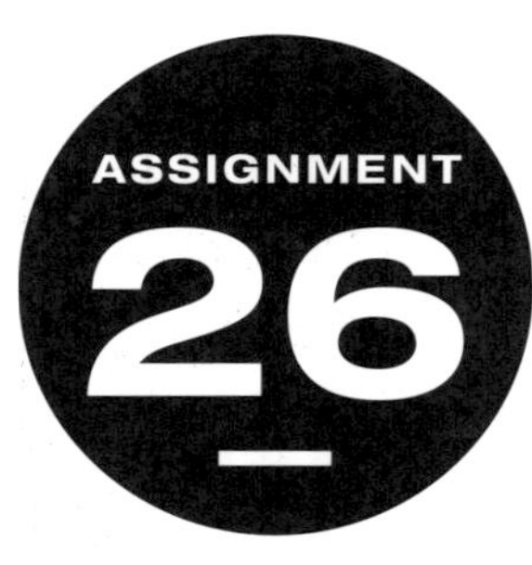

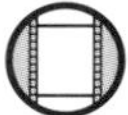

KIT LIST

- Medium-format film camera
- 35mm film
- 2 x small pieces of sponge
- 2 x hair ties or rubber bands

TIP

There are countless vintage medium-format cameras out there that use "obsolete" film formats, such as 620. However, they can still be loaded with 35mm film for your sprocket shots. Even better, they are generally cheaper to buy on eBay than "usable" medium-format cameras that take 120 roll film.

SEE ALSO

Why not combine your sprocket shots with Holgaramas (Assignment 46) to create more "extreme" panoramic shots and/or transform the look of your film through cross-processing (Assignment 11) or redscale (Assignment 21).

SPROCKET SHOTS

Loading 35mm film in a medium-format camera lets you exploit every last millimeter of the film, up to and including the sprocket holes at the edges. It also lets you shoot panoramic images up to the width of the camera's format—so you'll be able to shoot 60x35mm shots on a square-shooting 6x6 format camera, 90x35mm panoramics on a 6x9 format camera, and so on.

▶ *The elongated format of a sprocket shot—in this instance 35mm in a vintage 6x7cm-format camera—worked well with this tall composition. However, it proved impossible to keep things straight through the camera's tiny viewfinder.*

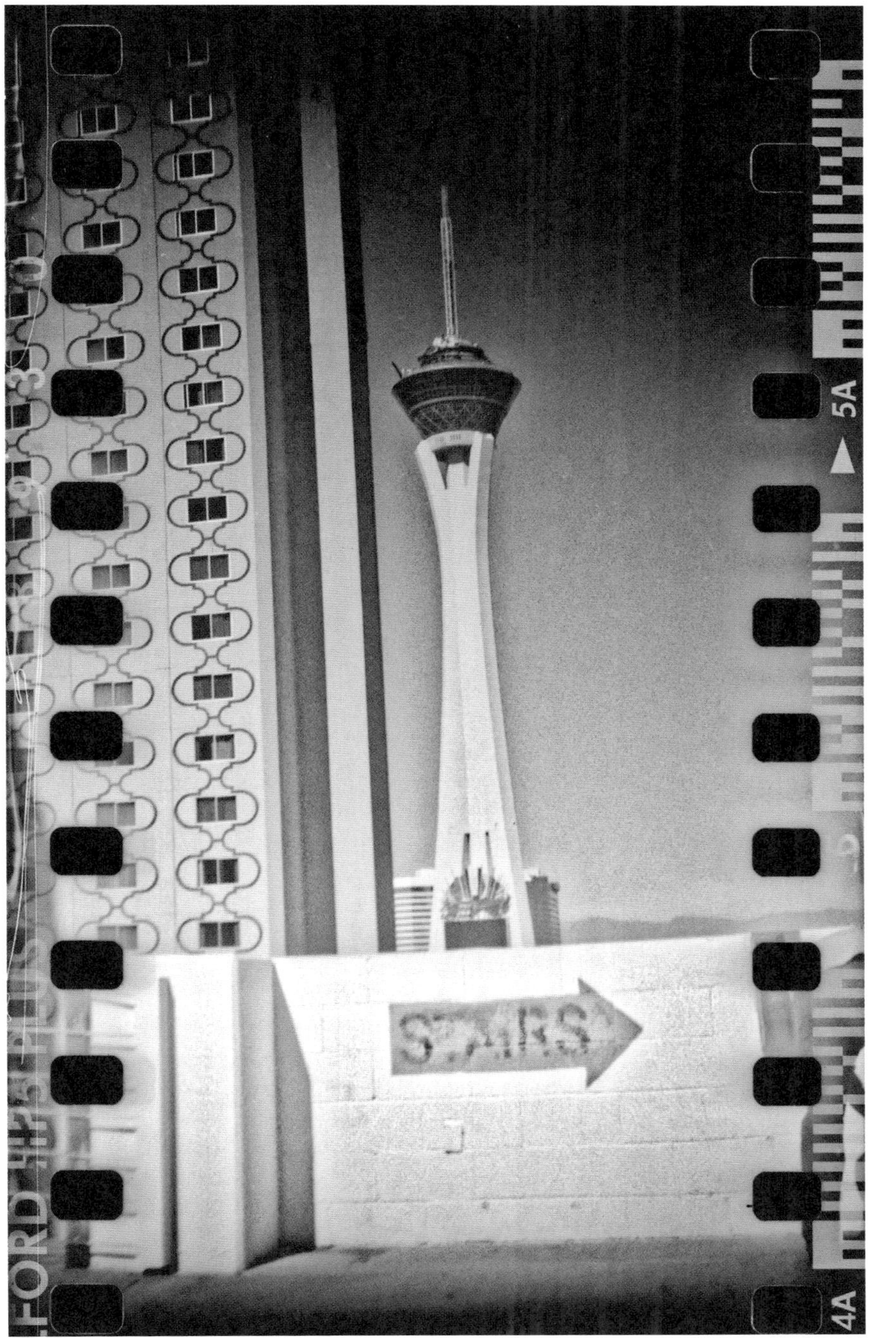
STARS

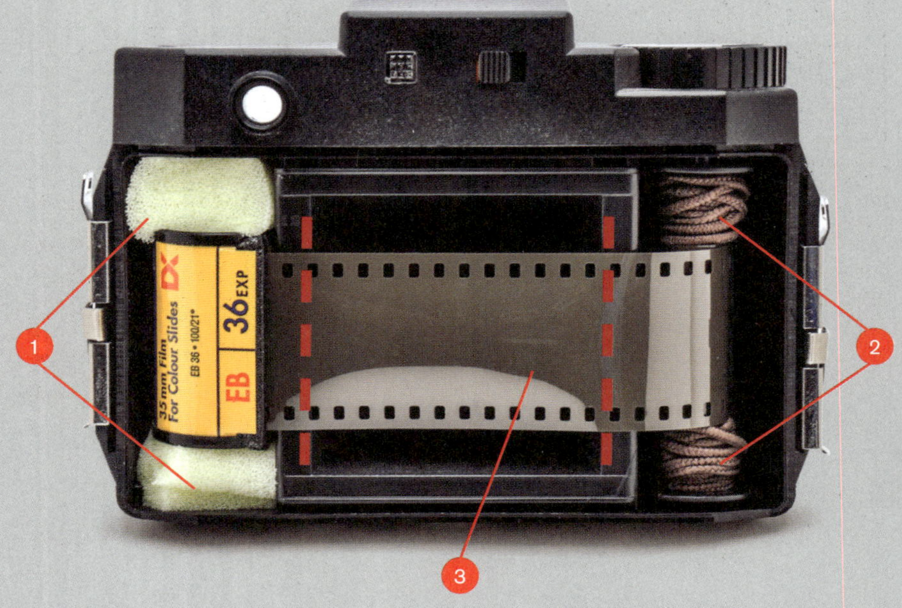

THE PROCESS:

1   Loading 35mm film in a medium-format camera is exceptionally simple. Start by putting your 35mm cassette in the camera and packing out the space above and below it with sponge.

2   You'll wind your 35mm film onto a regular medium-format spool. Wrap hair ties (or rubber bands) around the top and bottom of the spool to keep your smaller film in the center as it winds on.

3   Loading your film is now similar to loading a regular 35mm camera: drag the film from the cassette to the take-up spool, and then wind it on a few times, before closing the back and shooting as normal.

WINDING ON

Winding your film on can be challenging if you can't rely on the camera's usual frame counter. A simple way around this is to load a scrap roll of film, and shoot, and wind on with the back of the camera open.

Load the scrap roll and mark the edges of the first frame (as shown in red in the illustration). Then, wind the film on so the marks at the left are at the right of the frame. Make a note of how far you turned the camera's winding handle or crank.

Mark the new frame and repeat the process. You should soon get a rough idea of how far you have to wind between frames.

WARNING!

When you get to the end of your film you won't just be able to rewind it like you can with a regular 35mm camera. Instead, you'll need to unload the camera in the dark (in a changing bag or darkroom) and manually wind the film back into the cassette.

ASSIGNMENT JOURNAL

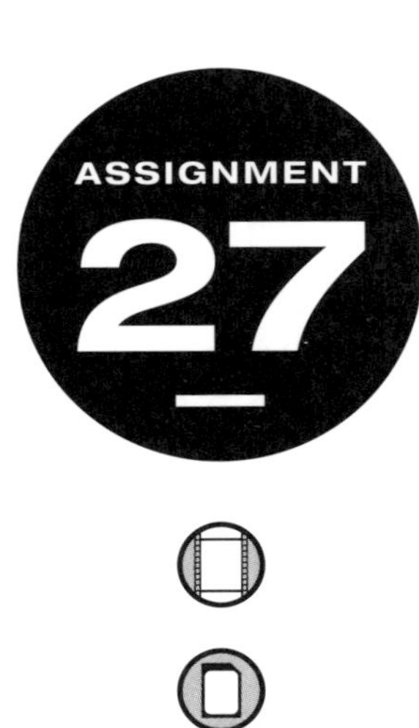

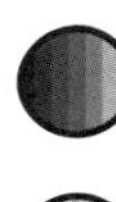

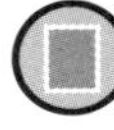

KIT LIST

- Any type of camera (including cameraphone)
- Tripod (optional)

TIPS

- You can create a coherent series of cloudscapes by targeting one cloud type—cumulus or cirrus, perhaps—or clouds of a similar size or shape. Keep your eyes open for the perfect opportunity.

- You could pick a specific time for your cloudscapes (sunset and sunrise are the obvious choices) or a particular meteorological event, such as a retreating weather front or storm clouds rolling in.

- It's easy to lose the highlights in a cloudscape, so set your exposure for the highlights: this might mean deliberately underexposing your shots.

CLOUDSCAPES

This is less an experiment and more a project that can be approached using a wide range of experimental techniques. It doesn't matter if you want to lie on top of a hill with a big sky all around you or find a patch of sky between city skyscrapers—just turn your camera skyward and photograph the clouds above. However, think about the experiment(s) you want to pursue. Maybe you want to create a giant joiner (Assignments 22 and 23) from a single cloudscape, use multiple exposures to layer varying cloud forms (Assignment 19), fit a welding glass filter to transform the clouds' passage through the sky (Assignment 33), use dyes or tones (Assignments 28, 35, and 49), cross-process your film (Assignment 11), create a triptych (Assignment 50), or combine multiple experimental techniques.

Do whatever it takes to make the project "yours."

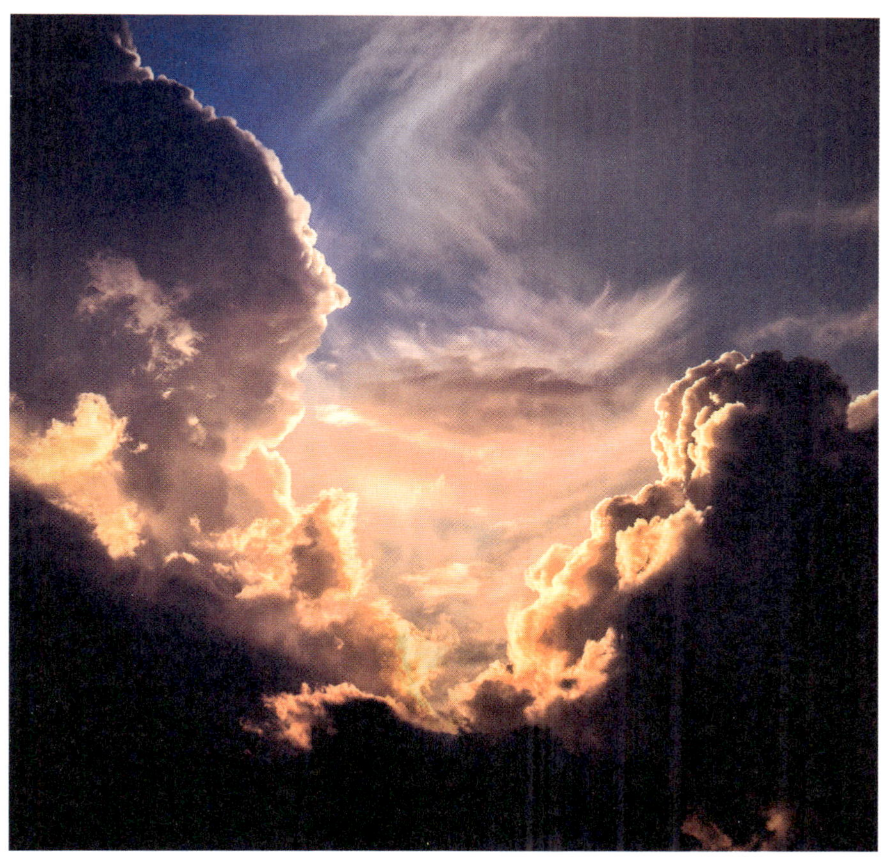

▲ *Make your cloudscapes your own: you might want to shoot dramatic skies at sunset and crop them square, for example.*

ASSIGNMENT JOURNAL

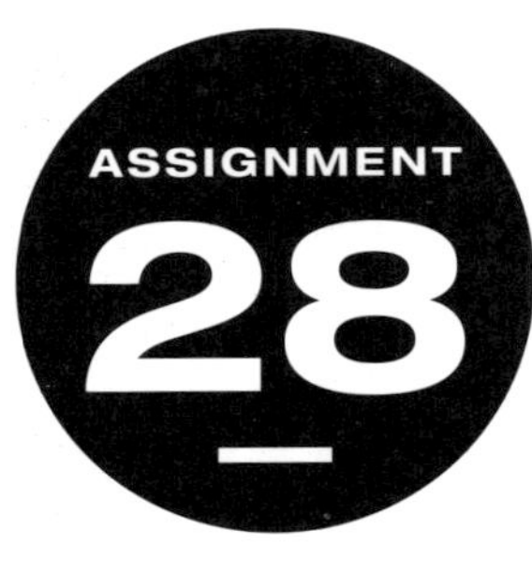

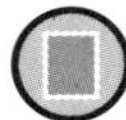

KIT LIST

- Black-and-white print
- Print tray or similar (to hold print)
- Tea

TIPS

- The ideal start point here is a traditional "wet" print made in the darkroom. However, digital prints made on heavyweight photographic papers may also work, so give it a go.

- Experiment with different types of tea to see how Earl Grey differs from Assam, for instance, or why not see if you can get creative with some colored herbal infusions?

- Vary the strength and temperature of the brew and adjust your toning times to control the intensity of the color.

- Build up a personal "tea toning" reference that you can go back to in the future.

- Don't like tea? Try coffee instead!

SEE ALSO

As an alternative to brown prints, take a look at the color-adding options in Assignment 35.

TEA TIME!

For years, darkroom practitioners have used strong tea mixes to tint and tone their images, creating myriad warm-hued prints along the way. The process is super-simple, super-cheap, and—compared to traditional darkroom chemicals—doesn't smell too bad, either. Simply fill a print tray with hot tea and slide your print right in. What you see is what you get, so just pull out the print when it's brewed to perfection.

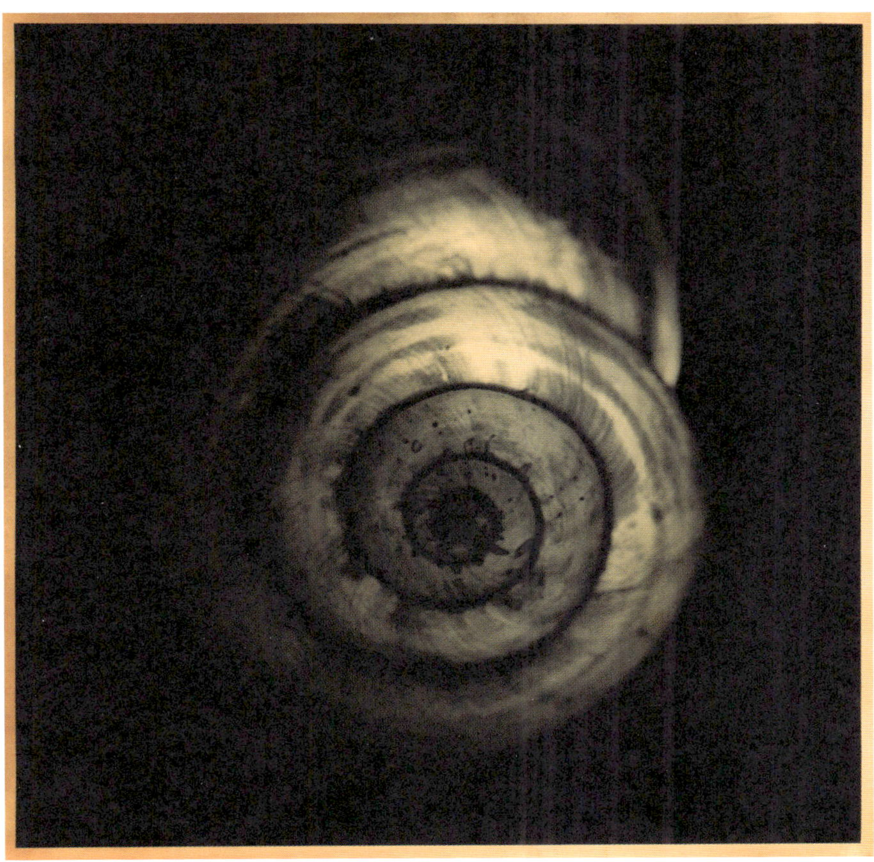

▲ *Tea toning isn't a precise science, so expect color variations across your print and uneven patches of tone—this is all part of the experimental effect!*

ASSIGNMENT JOURNAL

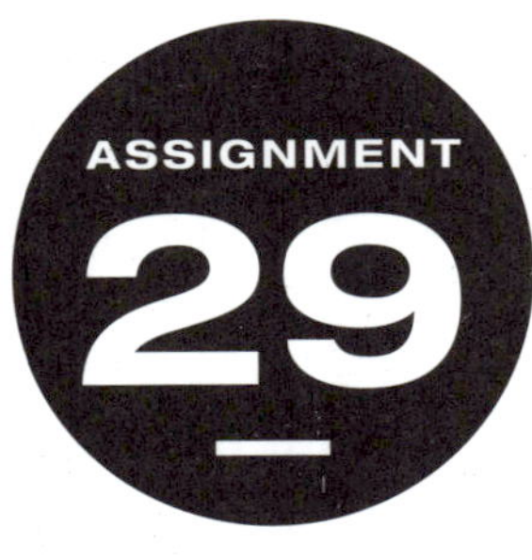

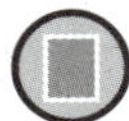

KIT LIST

- Prints (digital or traditional)
- Fire

TIPS

- Experiment with different types of paper: some will burn more quickly or slowly than others, and the construction of the paper will also affect how it reacts to fire.

- Vary your heat source and method of applying it—hold your print further from the flame for a "slow melt," or closer to it for an intense blast of heat.

- As well as prints, why not trying "cooking" your film. Remember this is a destructive process, though—there's no going back.

SEE ALSO

You could also try transforming your prints by soaking them in water (Assignment 14).

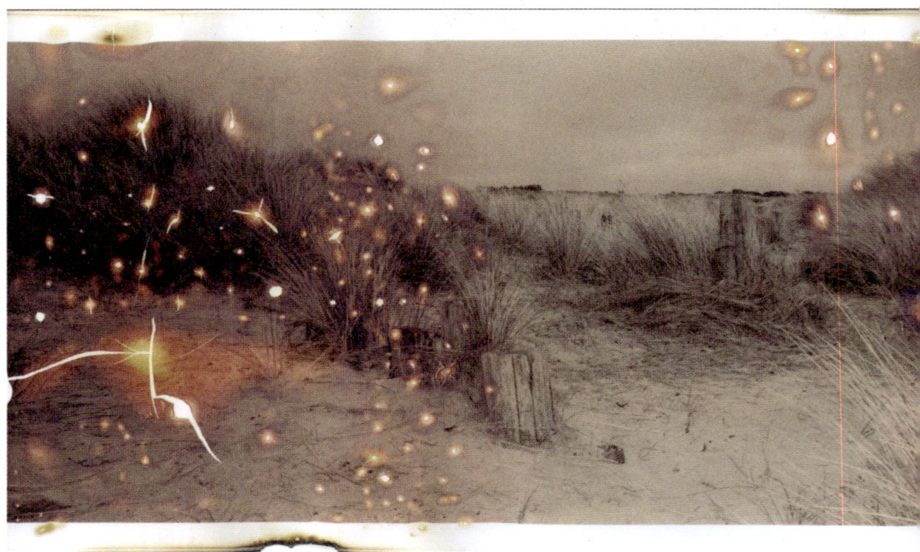

BURNING UP

There are countless ways of "abusing" your images, especially with image-editing apps. However, the ones that are most fun and also capable of producing the most interesting results are those that involve a "hands on" attack on your negatives or on your prints.

This experiment involves one of the most fundamental elements: fire! Whether it's matches, a blowtorch, or the sparks from an angle grinder, take a flame or some other form of extreme heat to your prints and see what happens.

Think about how a photograph's message can be changed when elements are charred or turned to ash.

ASSIGNMENT JOURNAL

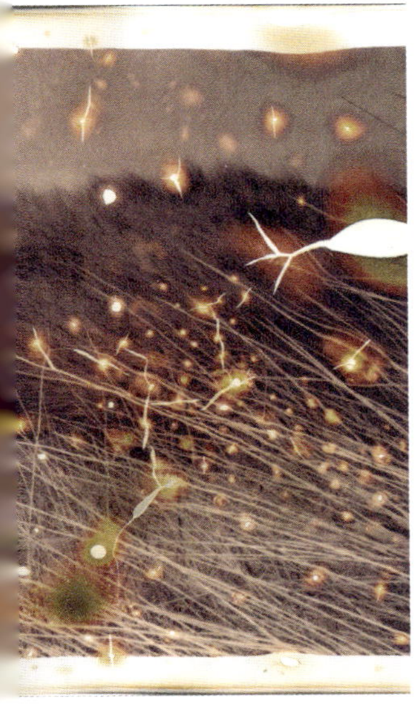

◄ *Holding this panoramic print over a gas stove "split" the emulsion, creating vivid cracks and splatters.*

WARNING!

It goes without saying that "playing" with fire is dangerous. If you're going to burn prints you need to do it somewhere safe (ideally outdoors), away from any sources of ignition, and make sure you've got a bucket of water, a hose, or a fire extinguisher at hand in case things start to go wrong . . .

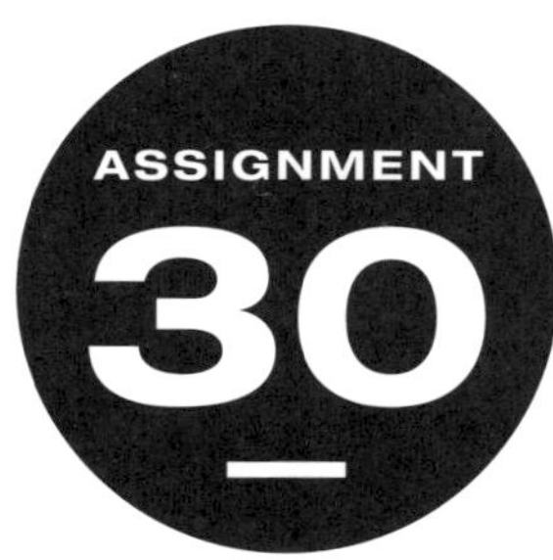

30

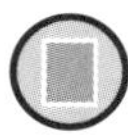

KIT LIST

- Prints
- Scissors or craft knife
- Glue

TIPS

- Emulate the "masters" of photomontage by removing the emulsion of the print from its paper backing. This will leave you with an ultra-thin image that will have less obvious edges when it's stuck down. Be warned, though—this isn't easy.

- The only limit to a photomontage is your imagination. Constructs can be realistic, surreal, or abstract—you simply need the vision to start with.

- Sketch out your ideas first, as this will make it easier for you to fine-tune the composition and work out which elements you need to source or shoot.

SEE ALSO

Peter Kennard is an artist who is renowned for political photomontages that include *Haywain with Cruise Missiles* (1980) and *Defended to Death* (1983). Head over to the artist's website www.peterkennard.com to find out more.

▼ *Cut-and-paste collages lend themselves to fantastical creations, so there's no need for your images to be restricted by "reality."*

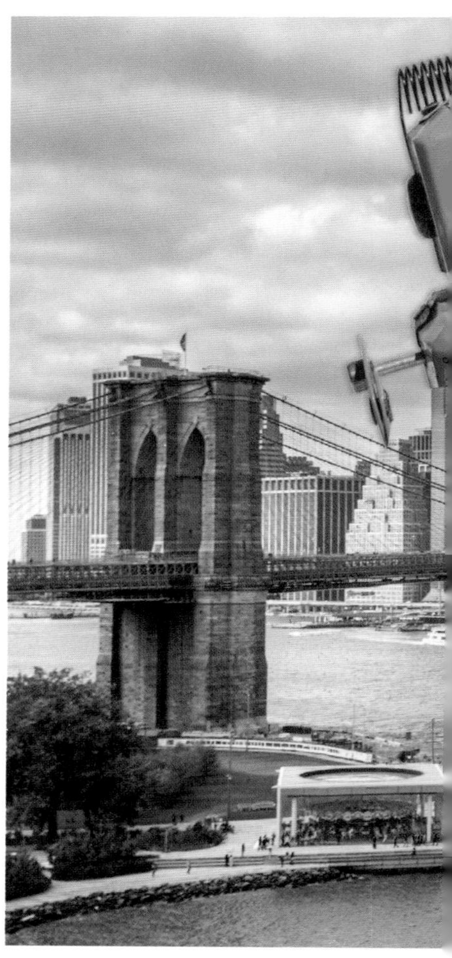

RIP 'N' STICK

Before the digital era, there were really only two ways you could combine elements from different photographs: you either shot multiple exposures (which could quickly become incredibly complex), or you cut out the elements from different prints and stuck them down to create your assembled image.

Although Photoshop has now made the whole "cut and paste" process real easy, old-school photomontages have way more character. So this experiment is simple: just grab some traditional prints (black-and-white, color, or a mix of both), reach for your scissors and glue, and start seeing what you can create!

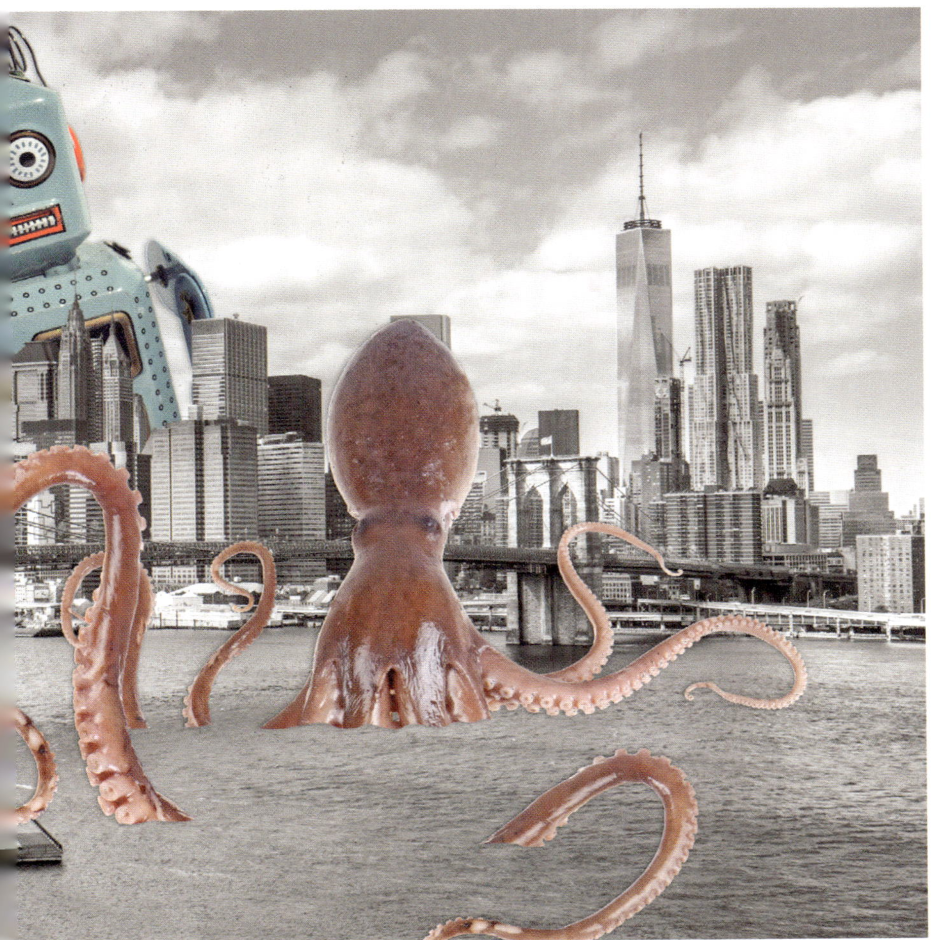

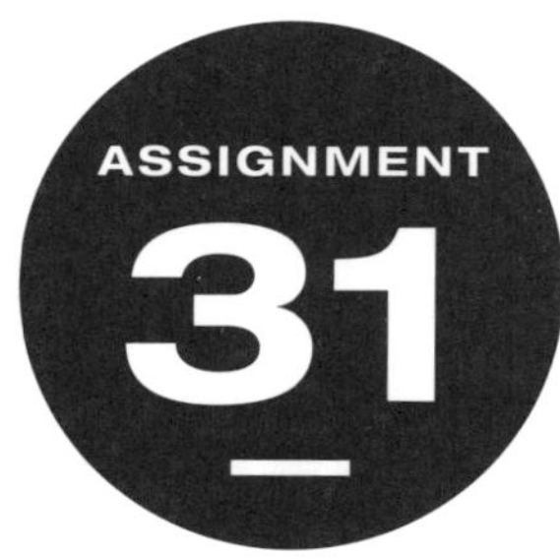

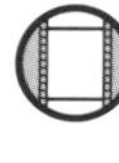
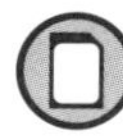

▼ *Silhouettes, rim lighting, and flare are all created when you shoot into the light.*

KIT LIST

- Any type of camera (including cameraphone)

TIPS

- The sun can wreak havoc with digital displays and sensors, so be careful with the framing of your shots (don't zoom in on the sun, for example). Film cameras are less sensitive.

- Modern lenses have multiple coatings designed to minimize and control flare, so for this experiment vintage lenses will actually perform "better" (i.e. your flare will be stronger).

SEE ALSO

Shooting through frosted (or wet) glass can also transform what your camera sees: head to Assignment 37 for details.

INTO THE LIGHT

Shooting "into the light" is a great way of creating striking silhouettes and throwing dramatic flare across your shots as the light gets bounced around on its way to your film or sensor. You don't need any special kit here: just position your subject with the light behind them and shoot. If your camera lets you, play around with your exposure setting to see what effect this has on the size and intensity of any flare, and look at how focus affects the image as well: defocused silhouettes with the light "eating" into the edges can be just as effective as a clearly defined subject.

WARNING!
NEVER look through your camera directly at the sun: at best it will hurt, at worst you'll irreparably damage your eyesight. It's just not worth the risk.

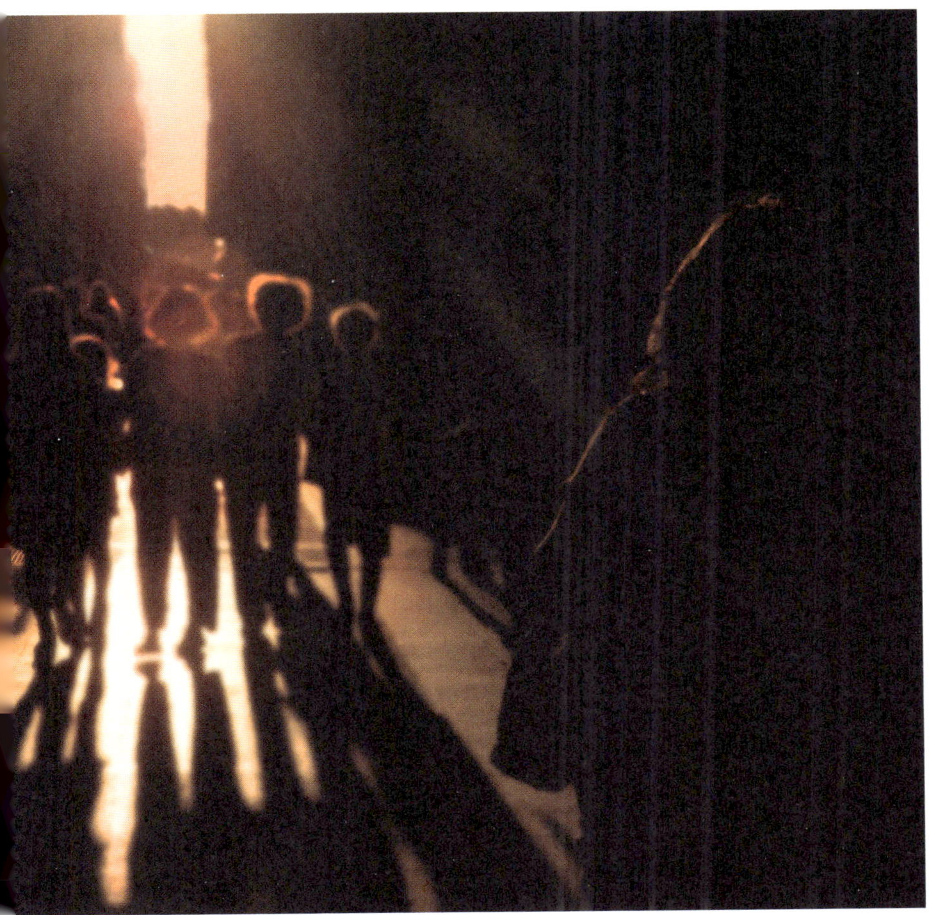

ASSIGNMENT

32

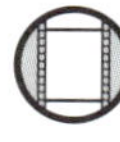

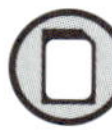

KIT LIST

- Any type of camera (including cameraphone)

TIPS

- Use a wide aperture to throw a foreground frame heavily out of focus, or a small aperture to keep things sharp from front to back in the image.

- Frames can be made up of different elements at different distances from the camera.

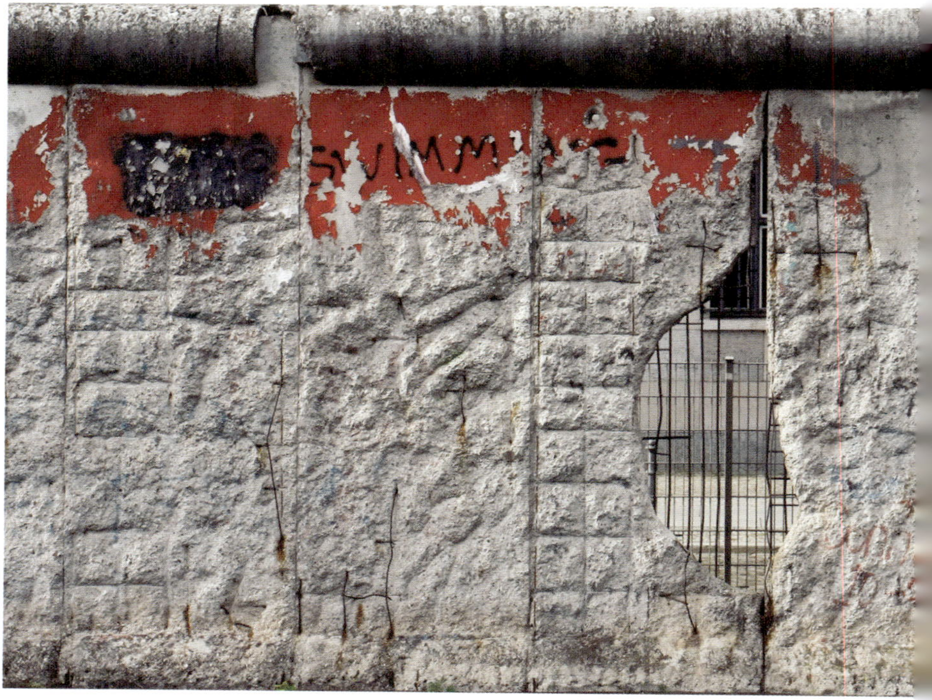

FRAMING

Framing your subject with elements around it is something that's straight out of "Composition 101." People framed in doorways or archways, buildings framed by the branches of a tree overhead, and portraits with the subject holding a picture frame in front of them are all pretty obvious examples of something that's been done to death. So why have it here?

The simple answer is this: it might be a "classic" way of framing (literally) a shot, but it's also an incredibly successful and effective one. So, forget the clichés and experiment with your own framed shots. Look for gaps in walls that you can see through, chinks in fences, holes in fabric, or anything that can be used in some way to frame and "hold" your subject.

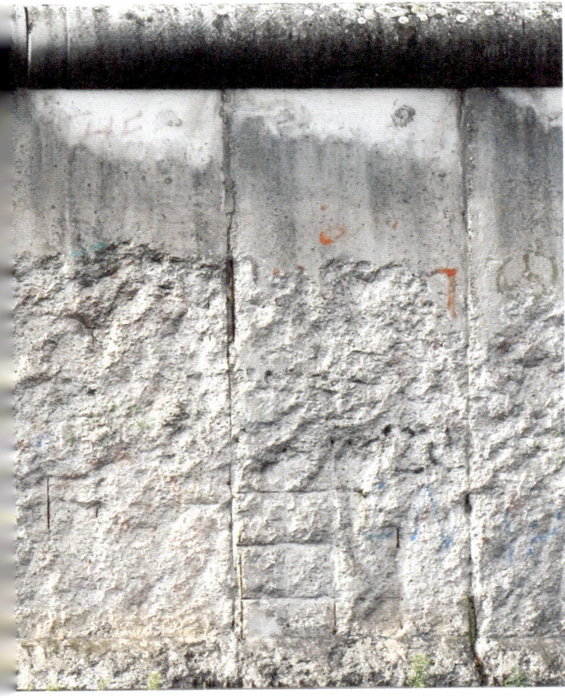

◄ *Framed shots don't have to be obvious. In this shot, the glimpse through a gap in the former Berlin Wall tells a far more emotive story than a fuller image would—it's all about a stolen glimpse of another world.*

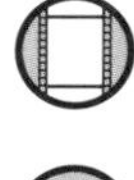

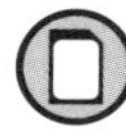

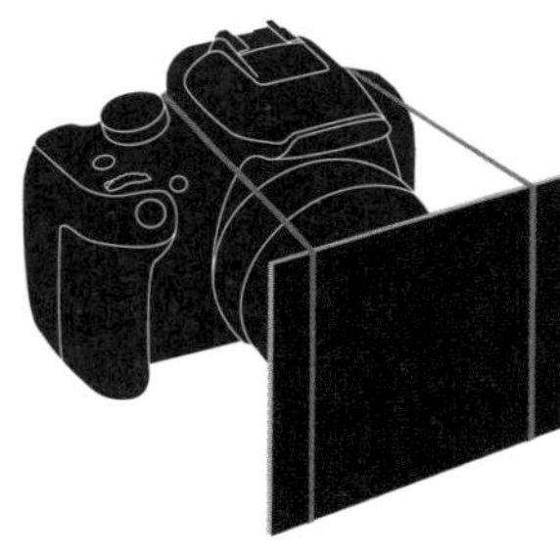

$1 ND FILTER

Neutral Density (ND) filters are like sunglasses for your camera—they reduce the amount of light reaching your film or sensor and increase the exposure time so you can create stunning long-exposure photographs. "Extreme" ND filters take it a step further and really let you drag your exposures, and, in doing so, the roughest sea can be calmed, clouds turn to mist, and people simply disappear from your photographs if they're moving. The downside? You need $100+ to get yourself an extreme ND filter. Or do you...?

A welding lens (designed to fit in a welding mask and prevent "arc eye") does pretty much the same job as an ND filter and you can pick them up for as little as $1. Sure, it's not "optical quality" (don't expect tack-sharp results for a dollar) and there are going to be some pretty strong color casts to contend with, but if you just want to experiment with long exposures without breaking the bank, give it a go.

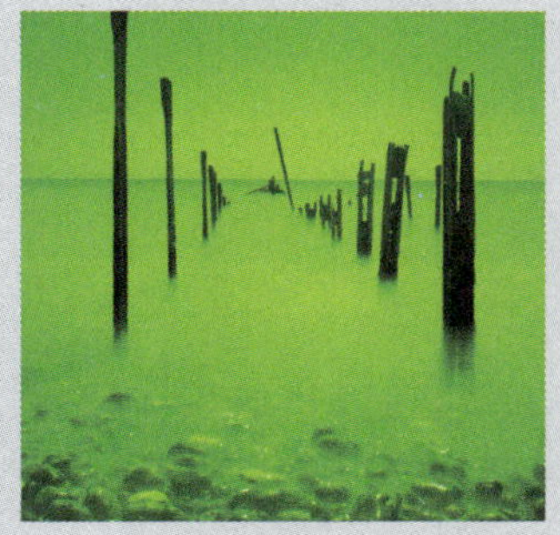

THE (SHOOTING) PROCESS

Shooting through a welding lens (or extreme ND filter) is slightly different to taking a "regular" shot. So, once you've set up your camera, follow these simple steps:

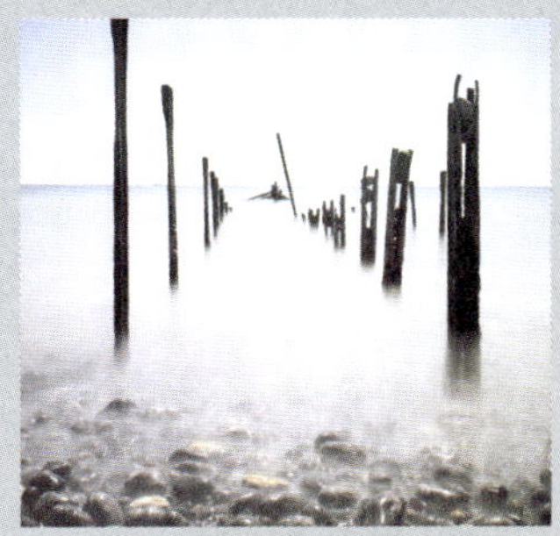

1 Your camera's AF won't see through the welding lens, so you'll need to focus manually before you attach the filter.

2 Still without the welding lens fitted, take an exposure reading and set the exposure in Manual mode. Then (and this is important) adjust the shutter speed to compensate for the lens—if the welding lens reduces the light by 5 stops, increase the shutter speed by 5 stops.

3 Attach your filter, taking care not to knock the camera or shift focus. Now you can shoot...

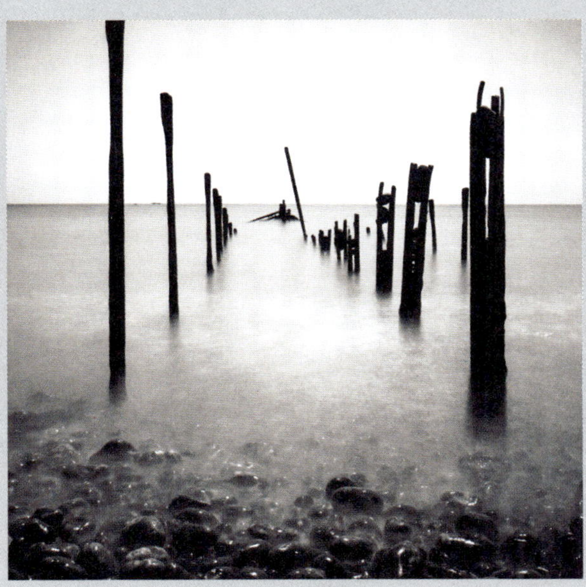

◄ *This shot was taken through a welding lens, which extended the exposure by 14 stops. Out of the camera the image has a strong color cast (top). Although this can be "dialed out" (middle), monochrome conversions can be more striking (bottom).*

KIT LIST

- Inkjet printer
- Paper to print on

TIPS

- You need to be careful when it comes to running "non-standard" papers through a printer—there's always a risk that the paper will jam.

- Set a custom paper size to ensure your printer prints in the right place.

- Experiment with the print quality settings to control the amount of ink laid on the page.

- Make sure your print is dry before you handle it. You may even find that the ink won't penetrate some glossy surfaces, so it won't dry at all.

SEE ALSO

Like a photomontage (Assignment 30), this is a much less conventional way of communicating a message.

ILLUSTRATED TEXT

Words and pictures are inextricably linked. When you read a novel, pictures are created in your head. Look at a photograph and you'll use words to describe it or the feelings that it evokes.

Use this experiment to take things a step further by printing directly onto text: tear pages out of a novel or cut out newspaper stories to form the paper you print on.

Alternatively, work it the other way and rip pictures from magazines to print words on.

In either case, you might decide to work on a literal level, using your picture to illustrate the text (or vice versa), or you might want to combine the two to create a deeper message.

try to rob us. Everything can be taken from you, if you let it be taken, Russell. I only figured out later who I should be aiming guns at. I guess if you survive you're bound to learn a few things.'

I heard her move closer and then I didn't hear anything. The old woman started belching. There were explosions on the TV. 'I know things are automatic for you,' Angie said. She was very close to me now. I could smell the gin and perfume. 'Have you ever committed a crime of passion, Russell? Have you ever taken a swing at somebody for the sheer meanness of it? Some of us try to do what's right and others do what's right for them. God doesn't favor either one, Russell – He just watches to see what the outcome is.'

She pushed the nozzle of the gun up against the base of my head and I closed my eyes. I tried to connect up what had led to where but I lost track like always. My death would yield up no more clues than anything else had. There would be no aggregation of events, no summary, no life flashing before my eyes, no benevolence or hatred. Just the sound of my own breath being muffled in a carpet and the music from a commercial playing in another room. I tried to lift myself up but couldn't; the gun kept me suspended there, like a butterfly stuck on a pin. Then I said something without thinking, without calculating even its general effect.

'I want to feel bad,' I told her.

And if I'm dead now while I'm telling you all this, then the transition from life was incredibly smooth. Angie took the gun away and started to cry, and when I opened up my eyes again I saw the little

▲ *Graphic images on a white background work particularly well for this experiment. I shot this semi-transparent waterpistol on a lightbox and then printed it onto the page of a crime short story.*

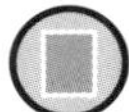

KIT LIST

- Prints
- Print trays
- Inks, dyes, or other "stains"

TIPS

- As well as inks and dyes, explore less obvious "stains" to work with as well, such as red wine and other colored drinks/fluids.

- Don't just stick to a single color: maybe experiment with "marbling" your paper using specialist inks?

- Don't use your best print trays for this experiment as the dye could ruin them. Aluminum roasting dishes are a great low-cost, near-disposable alternative.

SEE ALSO

Tea toning (Assignment 28) is another great way of adding color to a print.

DIP 'N' DUNK COLOR

Ink, fabric dye, watered-down paint—all of these things (and more) can be used to "stain" black-and-white prints. Simply line up some containers with your coloring agents and dip and dunk your prints. When they're ready, hang them up to dry.

Traditional darkroom prints are the ideal start point here, but inkjet prints made on heavyweight paper can work just as well. Keep experimenting to find out what works and what doesn't, and find your own experimental style.

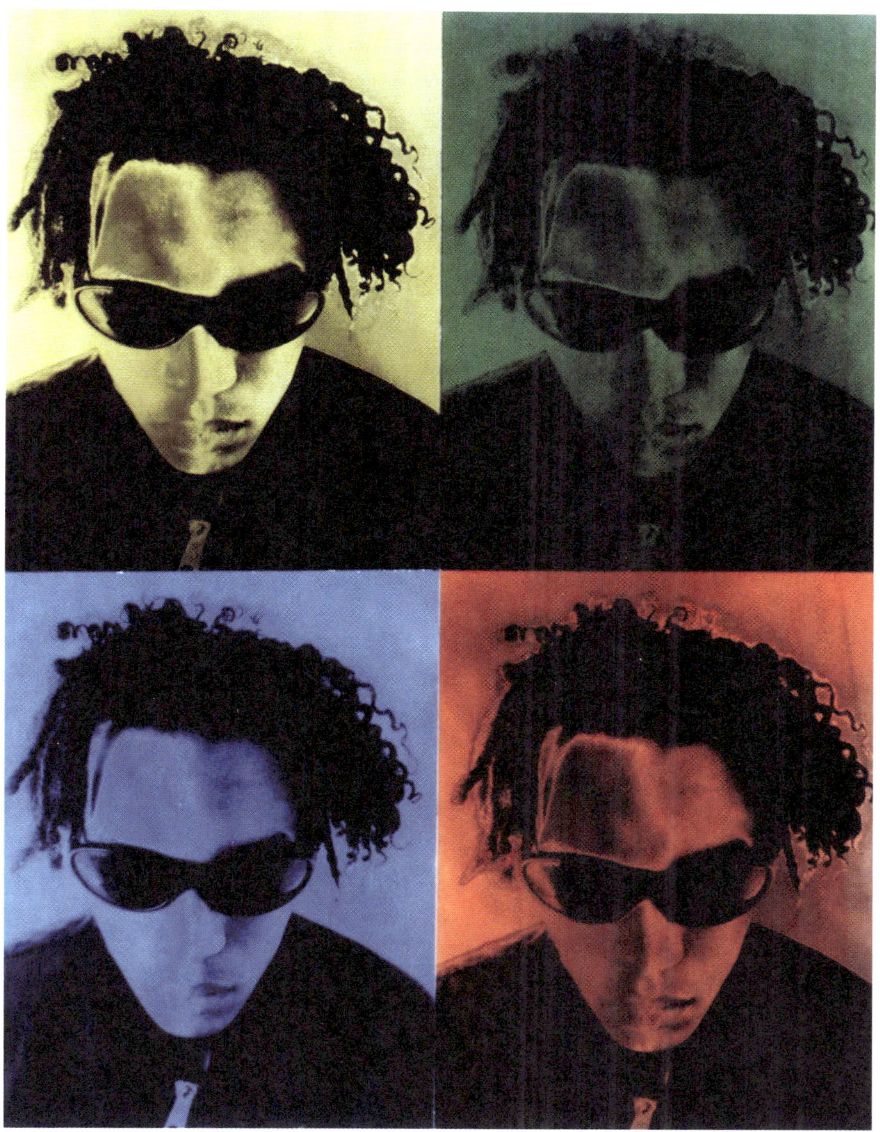

▲ *This experiment used fabric dyes to stain four solarized black-and-white prints different colors, before I assembled them in an Andy Warhol-esque grid.*

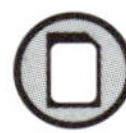

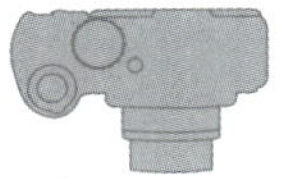

digital camera

KIT LIST

- Digital camera (any type, including cameraphone)
- Medium-format film camera with waist-level viewfinder
- Heavy card stock
- Scissors and tape

TIPS

- Unless you want to use your medium-format camera to shoot film with, look for a camera that uses an "obsolete" film format such as 620, as it will usually be less expensive. You can also use a camera with a broken shutter (cheaper still) as it's only the viewfinder and viewing lens you need.

- A point-and-shoot digital compact camera is ideal for your TTV experiments—you don't need a full-blown SLR.

- Make sure the film camera's viewfinder fills the frame of your digital camera: some digital point-and-shoot models can focus to less than an inch, but might not cover the full viewfinder frame at that distance.

- Use black electrical tape or gaffer tape to make sure the seams on your contraption are light tight; painting the inside flat black will minimize any internal reflections.

- Don't settle for "box brown"—paint and decorate the outside of your contraption!

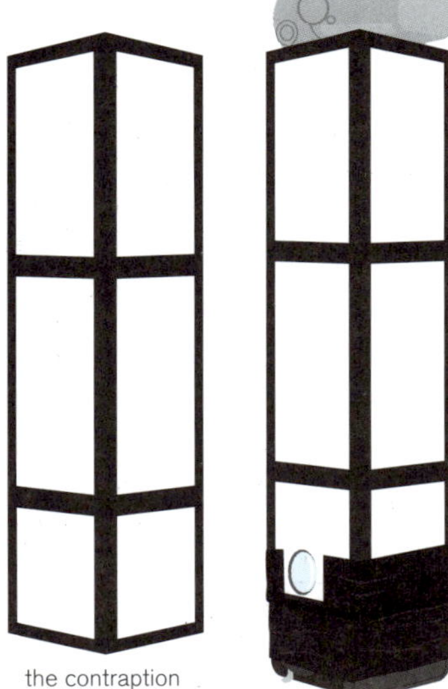

the contraption

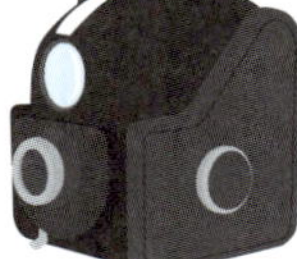

medium-format camera

◀ *"The contraption" is a light-tight conduit between old and new technologies. In this instance, thick card was used to create a square tube between a point-and-shoot digital compact and a vintage Ensign Ful-Vue.*

TTV

TTV, or "Through-The-Viewfinder" photography, is a great way of taking all the benefits of digital technology and combining them with the beautiful idiosyncrasies of vintage analog cameras. The idea is simple: you take an old medium-format film camera with a waist-level viewfinder and use a digital camera to photograph its viewing screen. In an instant you capture the medium-format camera's retro view of the world through its "primitive" viewing lens and imbue your digital shot with the dust, scratches, vignetting, and other artifacts that come with age.

At the heart of the process lies what is known as "the contraption," which serves as a light-tight conduit between the old and new technologies. Essentially, this is nothing more than a card tube: one end attaches to the top of the film camera, ensuring the viewing screen is in total darkness, while the other end has a hole in it for your digital camera's lens to poke through.

How you make your contraption is entirely up to you, but corrugated card is perhaps the cheapest and easiest option. The key thing is that the length of the contraption is at least the same as the minimum focus distance of your digital camera—any shorter and you won't be able to focus on the film camera's viewing screen!

ASSIGNMENT JOURNAL

"THE CONTRAPTION" PROCESS

1 The length of the contraption needs to be at least the minimum focus distance of your digital camera plus the height of your film camera. So, if your digital camera focuses down to 8 inches (20cm) and your film camera is 4 inches (10cm) tall, your contraption needs to be at least 12 inches (30cm) long.

2 Construct a four-sided box out of corrugated card or thick card stock based on the length above. The sides need to match the front, back, and side measurements of your film camera and you also need to add a flap at the top to create a lid.

3 At the bottom of the contraption (where the front of the film camera will be), make a hole for its viewing lens to poke through. Note that this is the viewing lens, not the lens used to take a shot.

4 Make a hole in the lid for your digital camera's lens. This should be slightly larger than the diameter of the lens—any bigger and light can leak in around the lens.

5 Slide your film camera into the bottom of the contraption and use tape to hold it in place with the viewing lens peering out through its "window."

6 Shoot! Just point your film camera at your subject, aim your digital camera down the contraption, and shoot the screen.

▶ *This pair of TTV shots were taken using the setup shown on the previous page. After cropping and processing, the images have a distinctly vintage look, complete with authentic dust, dirt, and scratches from the vintage camera's viewing screen.*

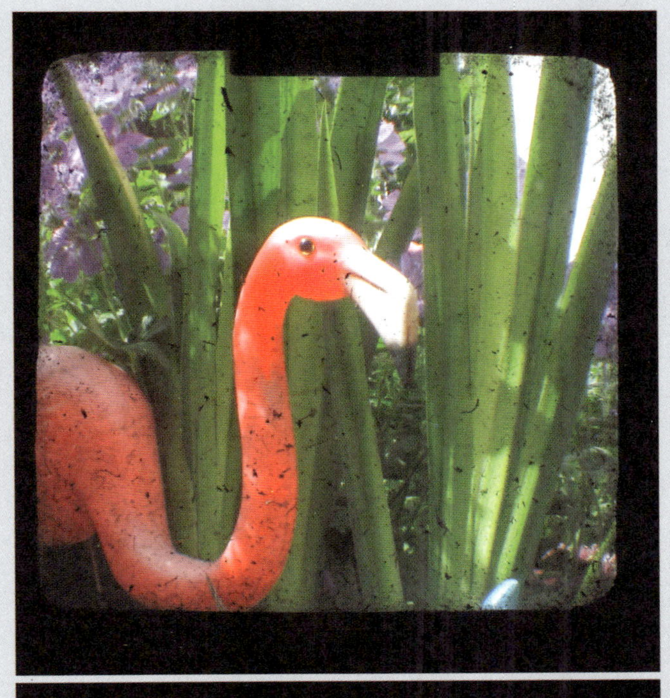

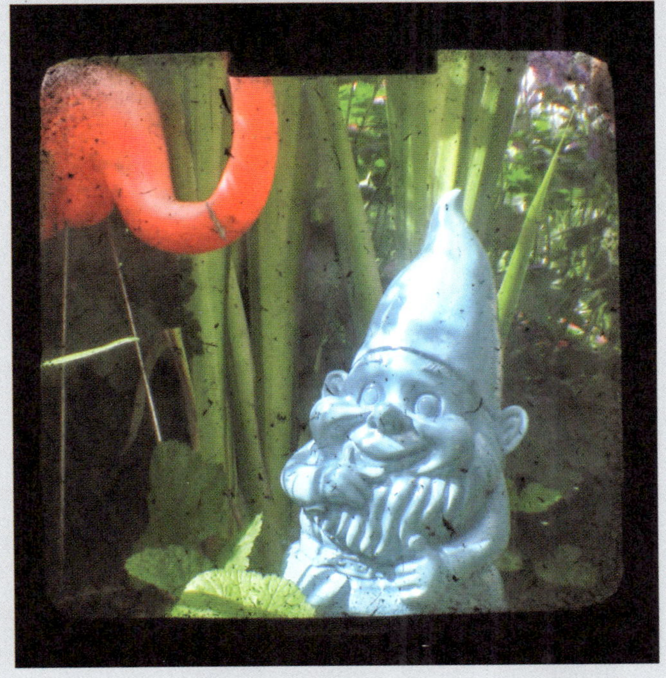

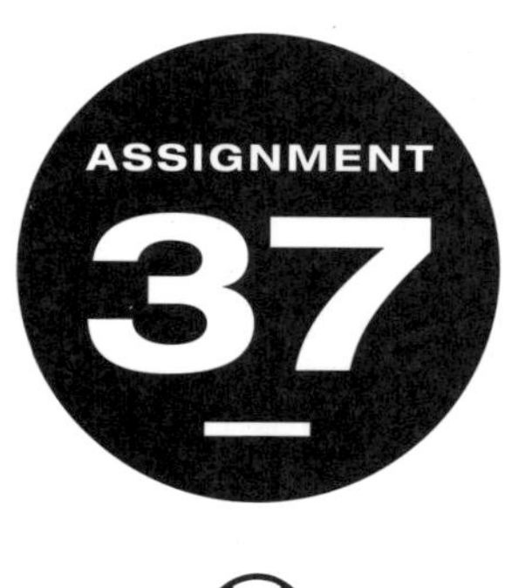

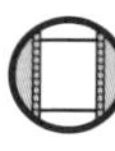
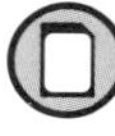

KIT LIST

- Any type of camera (including cameraphone)

TIPS

- Rain-covered windows can have a similar effect, depending on where you choose to focus (if, indeed, you focus at all).

- You don't have to wait until you discover some suitable glass to shoot through—give yourself more options by building up a set of textured glass filters using offcuts from your local glazier. (Remember, glass is SHARP, so tape up the edges!)

SEE ALSO

Plastic wrap (Assignment 20) is another great "front of lens" material for manipulating your subject, or you can simply defocus your shots entirely (Assignment 01).

TEXTURED GLASS

Add an element of mystery to your shots by photographing through textured or frosted glass. The textured surface will break your subject down into less distinct blocks of color and tone, which you can control through the camera-to-glass-to-subject distance and where you choose to focus.

▶ *The vertical pattern in this glass suited an upright (portrait) format image. The color was manipulated using the CameraBag 2 app.*

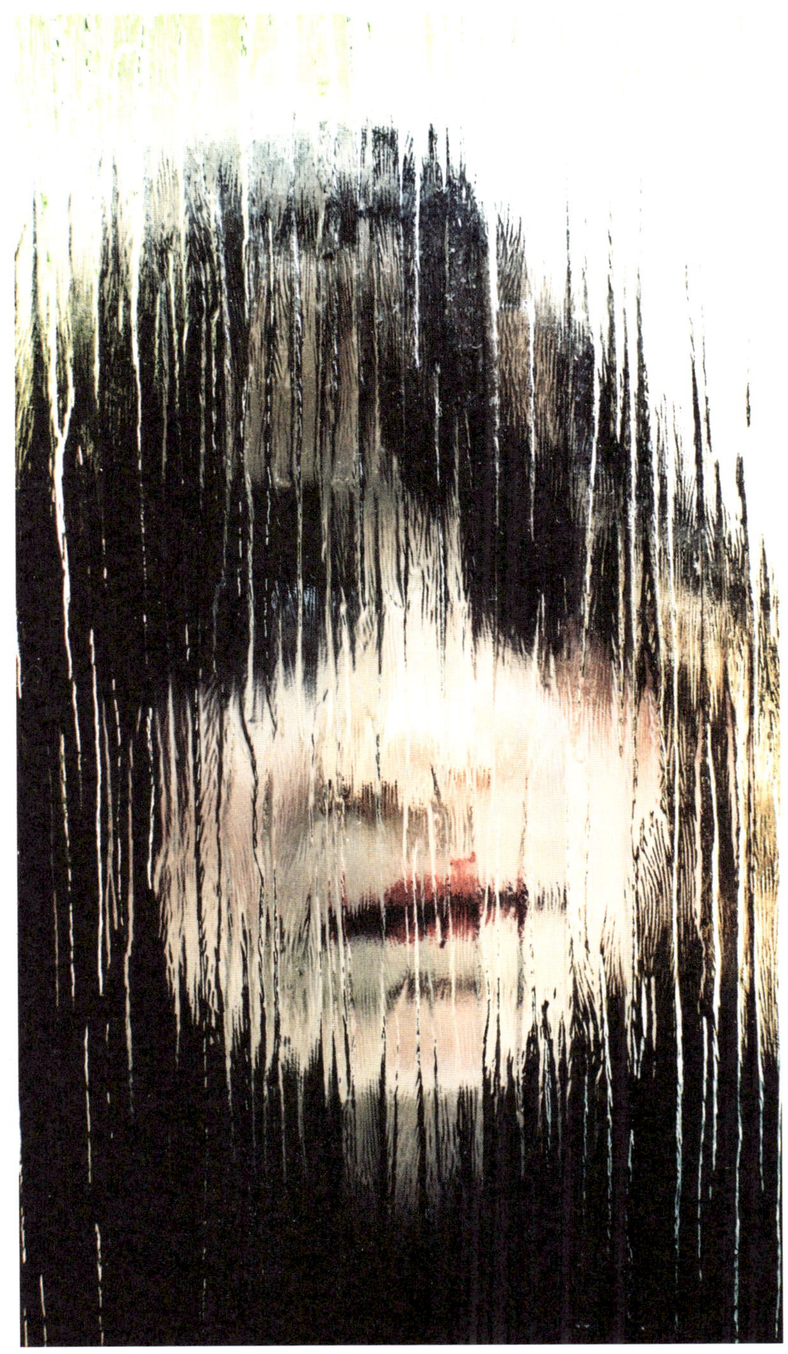

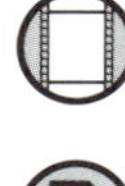

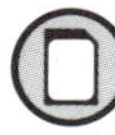

TIPS

- If you're working on a large scale, wear dark or black clothes and avoid staying still for too long or standing between your lightsource and the camera, otherwise you might appear in shot.

- Don't aim the light directly at the camera as this can create harsh hotspots.

- You can paint with light using a flash instead of a flashlight: set the flash to a low power output (if you can) and fire it multiple times around your subject to build up the illumination.

- Adding colored gels to your lightsource can transform your images—consider arming yourself with several filtered lights and switching between them as you paint your subject.

▶ *Unlike a straight shot with flash, painting with light enables you to selectively lighten parts of your subject, while letting others remain in darkness. It's up to you to decide where the light falls.*

KIT LIST

- Camera with manual exposure control
- Tripod
- Flashlight or flash

SEE ALSO

For an alternative approach to painting with light, check out Assignment 41.

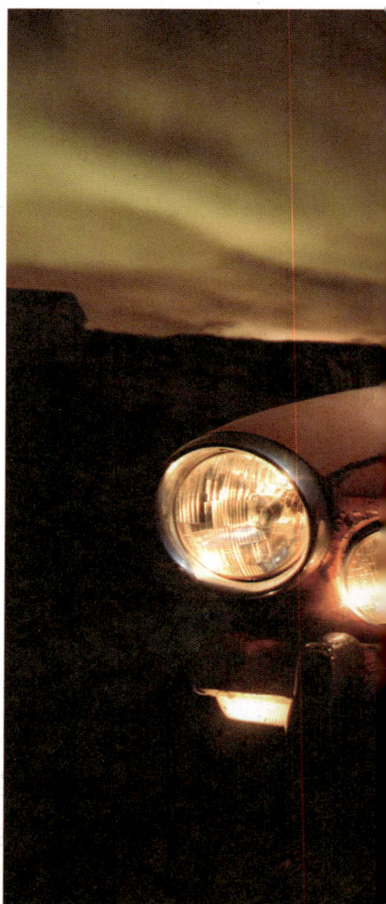

PAINT WITH LIGHT #1

This experiment involves the "classic method" of painting with light, which you can do indoors or out and on a small or large scale—the main thing is that it needs to be dark.

Set your camera up on a tripod and set a low ISO (100–200) and medium aperture (around f/8). This should give you a long exposure time—30 seconds is great, but don't be afraid to use your camera's "T" (Time) mode, or "B" (Bulb) mode if it has one, so you can manually open and close the shutter for super-long exposure times. Then, with the shutter open, just move your flashlight around your subject to "paint" it with light. The longer you hold the flashlight in a certain place, the brighter that part of your subject will be.

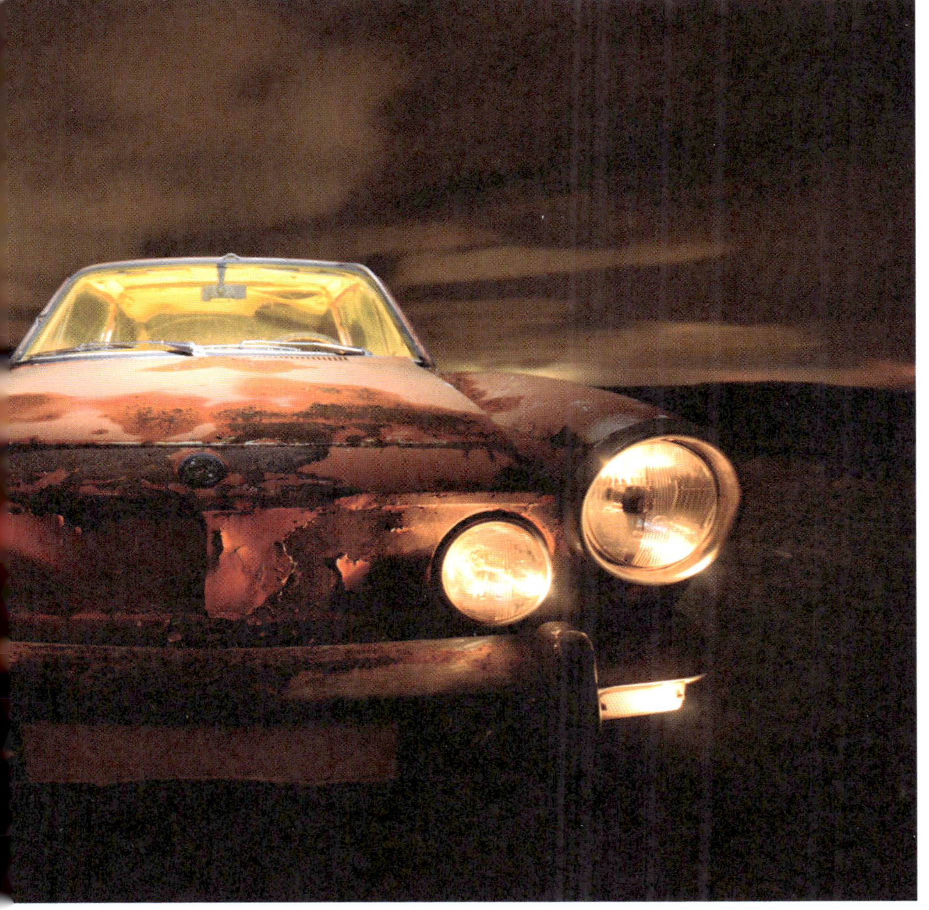

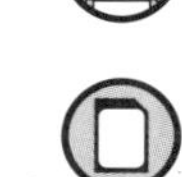

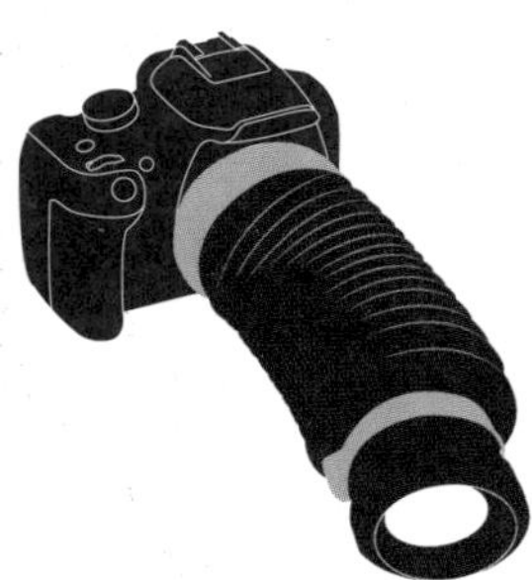

KIT LIST

- SLR or mirrorless interchangeable lens camera
- Lens with manual aperture control
- Lens mount
- Rubber fork gaiter
- Hose clamps

TIPS

- Enlarger lenses are perfect for this experiment, as they're cheap and plentiful.

- A medium-format enlarger lens (as used here) allows you to make more radical movements than a lens designed for printing 35mm film.

- You'll lose some light through the "body" of your lens, so be prepared to increase the exposure to compensate.

SEE ALSO

Freelensing is a zero-cost alternative to a tilt-shift lens—see Assignment 18.

TILT LENS

Want to experiment with tilt-shift photography? Can't afford the four-figure price tag of a premium lens for your SLR or mirrorless camera? Then, why not make your own out of a couple of low-cost parts?

There are countless ways of making your own tilt lens, with options including sink plungers and rubber tubing. Essentially though, it comes down to three key ingredients: a lens, a lens mount, and something with a bit of movement that you can fit between the two. The version shown above uses an old 5.3-inch enlarger lens (less than $10 on eBay), the end of a super-cheap extension tube for the lens mount (less than $10, new), and a rubber motorcycle fork gaiter (less than $5 for a pair). Even with a couple of hose clamps to hold it together the total cost was around $25—you might even be able to save on that if you've already got some of the pieces kicking around. Now you can start experimenting.

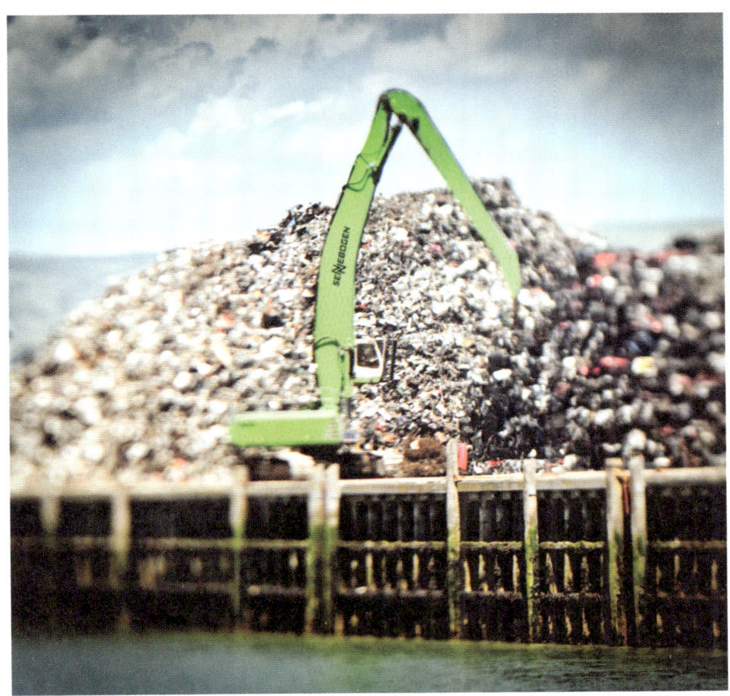

▲ *The focus in this tilted shot runs diagonally through the frame from top left to bottom right, creating a distinct "slice" of sharpness.*

THE (SHOOTING) PROCESS

1 You won't have any electrical connections between your camera and lens, so you'll need set your exposures manually. Be warned, though: smaller aperture settings will result in the image through the viewfinder or on the rear LCD becoming very dark as the lens "stops down."

2 Focusing relies on a combination of how far the lens is held from the camera and the camera-to-subject distance. The simple rule is that the further away the lens is from the sensor, the closer the focus distance.

3 "Tilt" the lens to manipulate the focus plane. This is where you can set the focus to slice sideways through the image. You'll likely have to tweak your focus as you tilt the lens, so the process becomes something of a juggling act and it can be tricky to get your subject sharp at first. Stick with it, though, and you'll soon get the hang of it.

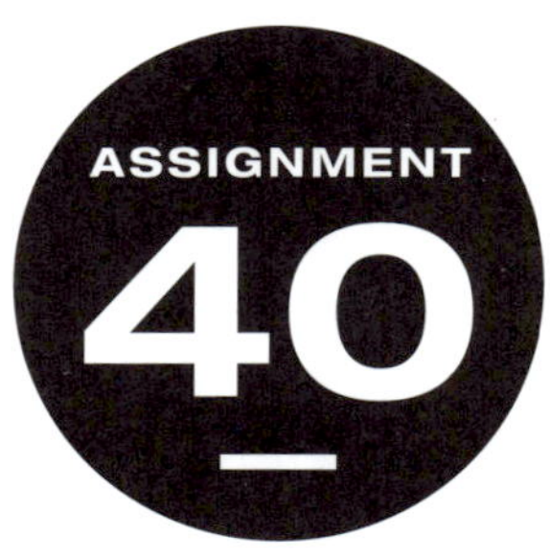

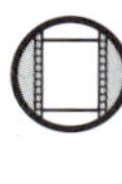

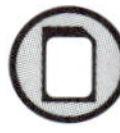

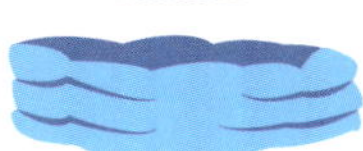

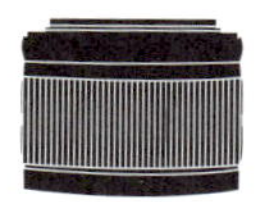

KIT LIST

- Interchangeable lens camera
- Manual 50mm prime lens (see Tips)
- Potato chip can
- Fabric
- Camera body cover (optional)

TIPS

- Because your lens isn't attached to the camera, you don't need to worry about it being the right fit. Look for a cheap 50mm prime from an "obsolete" system if you need to buy a lens, and pay no more than $10–20.

- You don't have to use a chip can—any light-tight tube that can be used to move the lens away from the camera body will do the same job.

- The longer your macro tube (chip can), the less light there is reaching your film or sensor. This means that you'll need to set a slower shutter speed or increase the ISO to compensate.

◄ *A chip can extension tube can be made any length. The main thing to remember is that the longer it is, the greater the magnification, but the less light there is reaching your film or sensor, so you may struggle to handhold your camera and lens without introducing shake.*

CHIP CAN MACRO

Macro extension tubes work on a really simple principle: as a lens gets further from the film or sensor it can focus much more closely than its regular minimum focus distance. However, you don't need dedicated extension tubes to make this happen—an empty potato chip can and a "nifty fifty" (50mm prime lens) is all you need.

As illustrated here, take your chip can and cut a hole in the base that's slightly larger than the lens opening on your camera. You can also cut the can down if you want to make it shorter (less magnification), but always cut from the top, rather than the base.

Next, take a manual 50mm prime lens, wrap it in fabric, and push it into the top of the chip can. You want a secure, light-tight fit.

Now, it's simply a case of holding your chip can tube tight against your camera and shooting. You'll have to set the exposure manually, and focus by moving the camera (or subject), but you can experiment with some "extreme" macro photography.

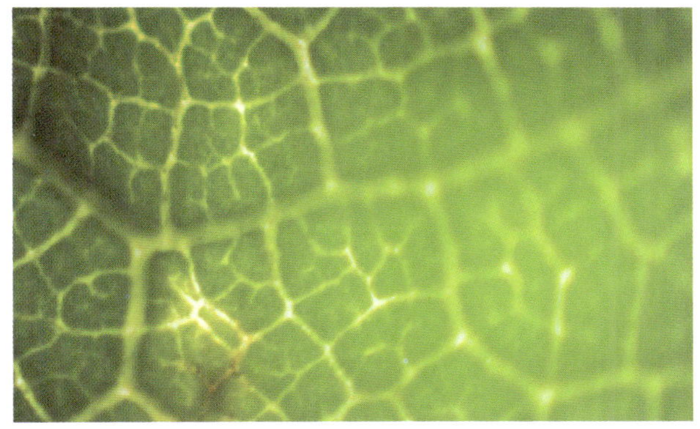

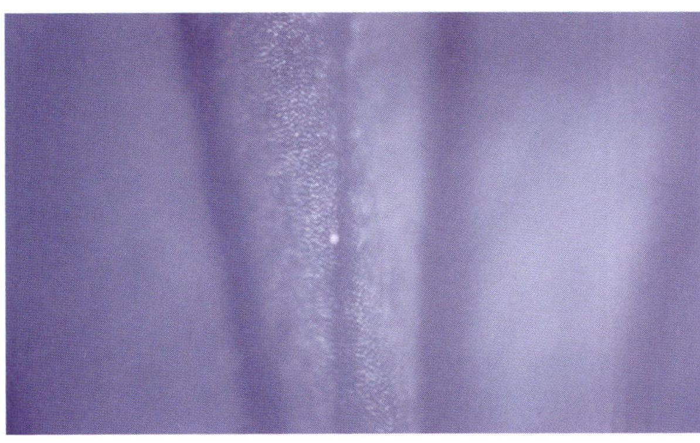

◀ *Chip can macro can enable you to get super-close to your subjects, transforming them into pure abstract images.*

ASSIGNMENT 41

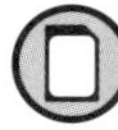

KIT LIST

- Camera with manual exposure control
- Tripod
- Light wand

TIPS

- There are many photographic light painting tools for you to choose from, but they can be hugely expensive. Instead, head to your local toy store and check out the lightsaber aisle for a source of low-cost colored light sticks!

- It can help if you have an assistant for this experiment—one of you can "perform" for the camera, while the other fires the shutter.

SEE ALSO

For a more traditional approach to painting with light, check out Assignment 38.

ASSIGNMENT JOURNAL

PAINT WITH LIGHT #2

This is the antithesis of Assignment 38. You're going to set up your camera in the same way; but this time, instead of using a flashlight (or flash) to illuminate your subject, use a light "wand" or illuminated poi balls to create dramatic light trail patterns. You can even try burning steel wool in front of the camera to get some truly stunning sparks.

"Dance" with your light weapon of choice. Wave it around without a care in the world and let organic shapes form on your film or sensor. And if a shot doesn't work? Just try again!

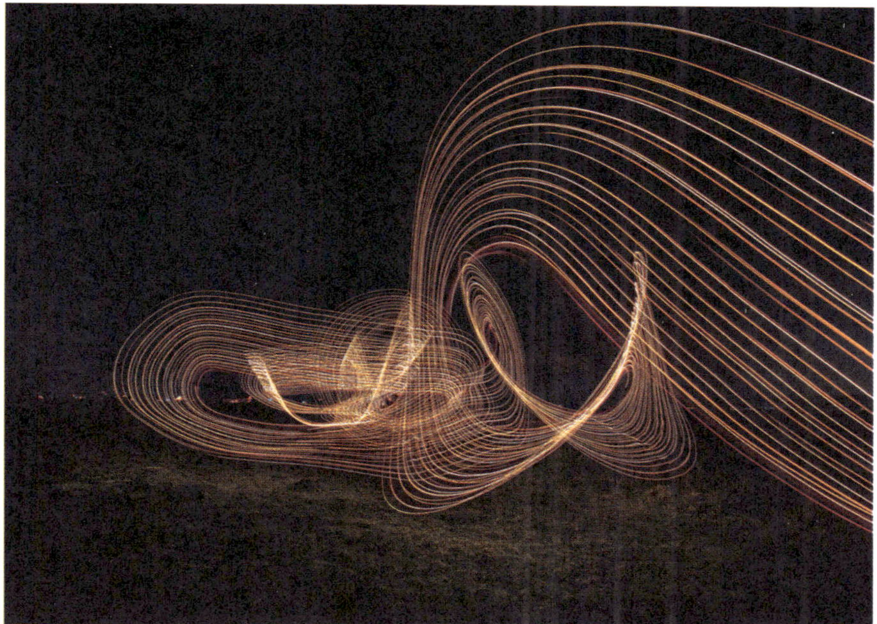

▲ *This experiment is all about creating abstract light trails in front of the camera, using anything from an expensive "pixel stick" to a toy lightsaber.*

WARNING!

Burning steel wool is dangerous—not only can it hurt you and your camera, but there's a very real risk you'll start a fire if you're near anything flammable. Use some common sense or leave well alone!

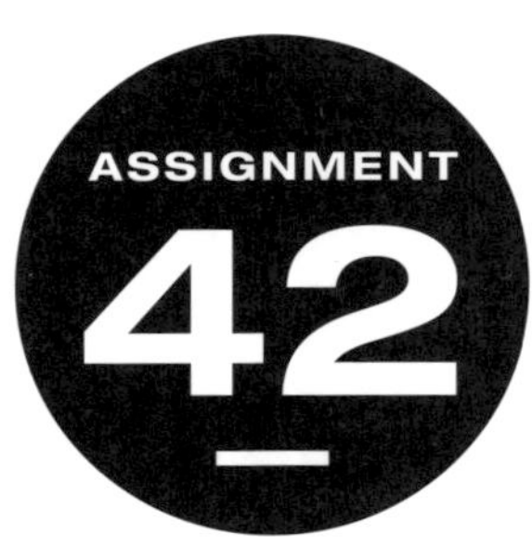

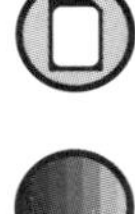

KIT LIST

- "Fast" telephoto lens
  (100mm+ with maximum aperture of f/2.8–f/4)
- Tripod (optional)

TIPS

- If your editing software doesn't have an automatic stitching tool you can combine your images by hand—be warned, though, it will take a lot of time.

- Using a tripod makes it a lot easier to ensure you cover the full area you want to shoot.

- If you're photographing a person you'll need them to hold still while you shoot your sequence. If not, you might find it difficult to line up your shots.

- Set your focus and exposure manually-- you don't want either one to change while you shoot.

SEE ALSO

Although you can use the Brenizer Method if you're shooting film, it can prove expensive and will involve the additional stage of scanning all your images. However, you could use it as the basis for a Hockney-esque joiner (Assignments 22 and 23).

BRENIZER METHOD

Credited to Ryan Brenizer (hence the name), the "Brenizer Method" is a style of photography that overcomes the laws of physics. Put simply, it enables you to combine the "compressed" perspective and shallow depth of field associated with telephoto lenses with the viewing angle of a wide-angle lens. How does it achieve this "magic?" The effect is created by combining multiple shots taken using a fast telephoto lens set at a wide aperture setting to minimize depth of field.

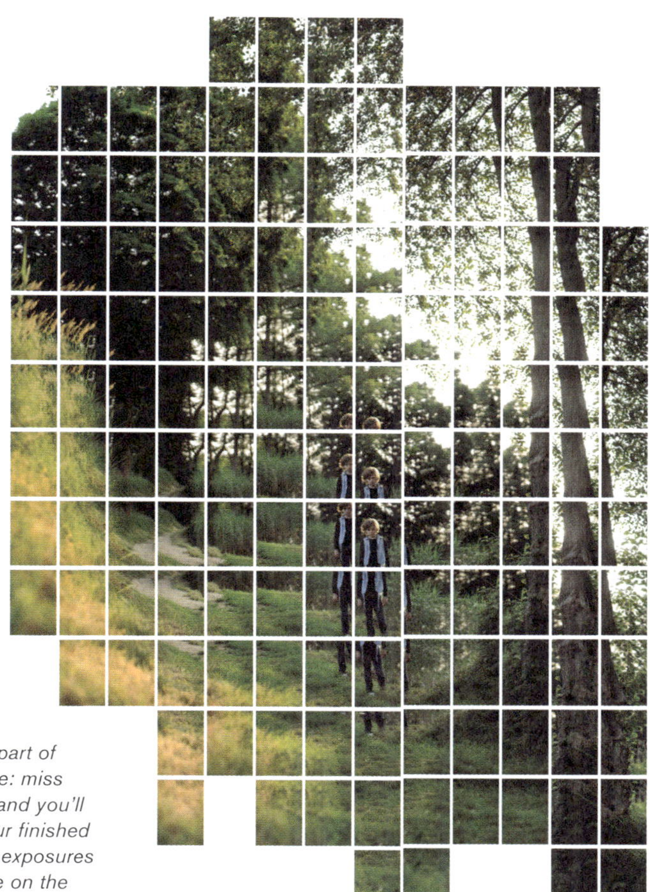

Just like shooting a stitched panorama, multiple frames are taken, and by working
both horizontally and vertically you can cover a wide viewing angle (a tripod really
helps here). All you need to do is ensure you cover the entire (wider) view that you
want, with plenty of overlap between your frames so they can be stitched together.
It often helps to work in a grid, starting at one corner and shooting a row of images
before raising (or lowering) the camera and shooting the next row, as illustrated here.
Then, it's simply a case of stitching your shots together...

THE (STITCHING) PROCESS

1   Copy your source images into a single folder on your computer and process them if they're Raw files.

2   In Photoshop, you'd use the Photomerge tool to combine your shots, but any editing program that has some sort of "auto-stitching" option should work. The aim is for the software to identify the overlapping areas in each of your images and assemble them into a single shot.

3   Once the processing has finished, you'll be left with a single Brenizer Method shot. It will likely need cropping to tidy up the ragged edges, but the effect will be there: a wide-angle view with telephoto "compression" and shallow depth of field.

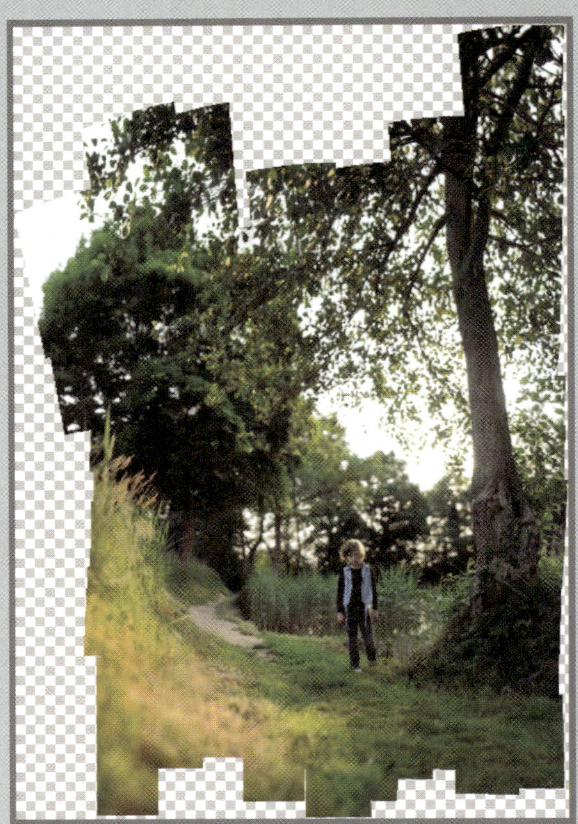

◄ *Processing a Brenizer Method image involves combining the source images. It helps if your software can do this automatically for you.*

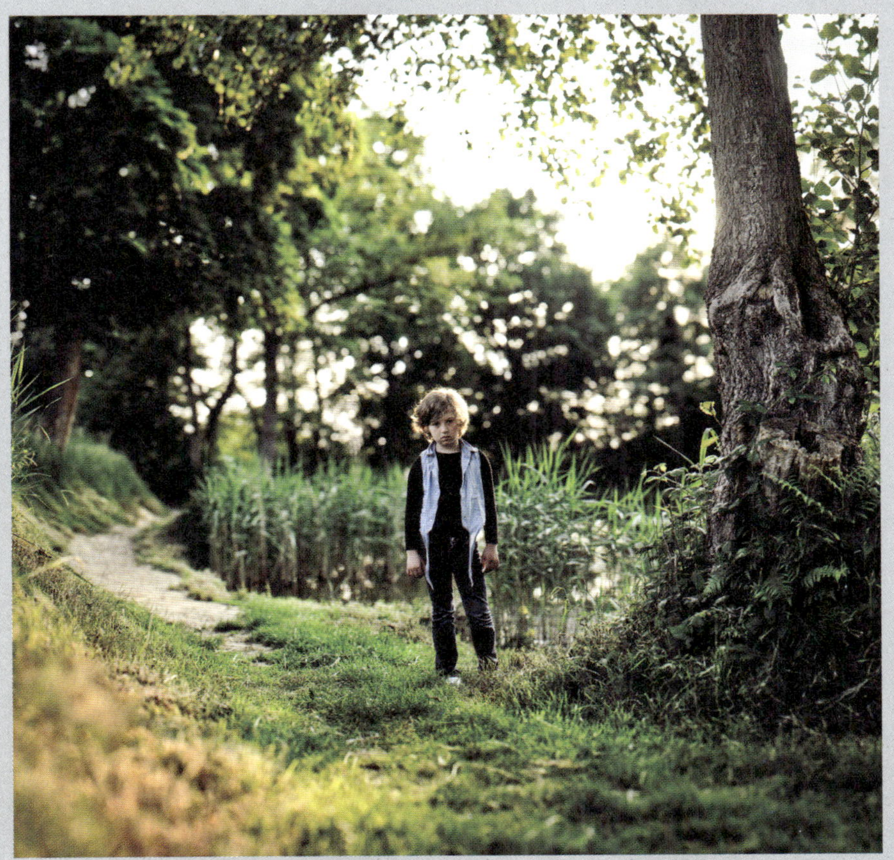

▲ *Once the exposures have been combined, the final image can be cropped and processed further. The result is a wide-angle view with telephoto depth of field (and "compressed" perspective).*

ASSIGNMENT JOURNAL

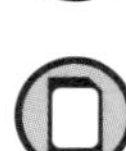

KIT LIST

- Any type of camera (including cameraphone)
- Projector

TIP

Working in a darkroom, try combining flash with a long exposure for your projected images—the long exposure will record the projected image, while the flash will momentarily light the surroundings. Be careful that the flash doesn't "drown out" the projected image, though—it's all about finding the right balance.

SEE ALSO

Back in the 1960s, fashion photographer John French (whose assistants included David Bailey and Terence Donovan) famously projected flowers and patterns onto his models to create "virtual" outfits: perhaps you can take his early experiments to the next level!

PROJECTED IMAGES

Projection photography is all about projecting images onto a subject (or object) and photographing the result. It's not a new technique, but digital projectors have now made it easier than ever to manipulate the images you project, as well as offering much more control over scale and brightness. All you need is a projector, a reasonably dark room, and a camera to record the results, and you're ready to start your experiments.

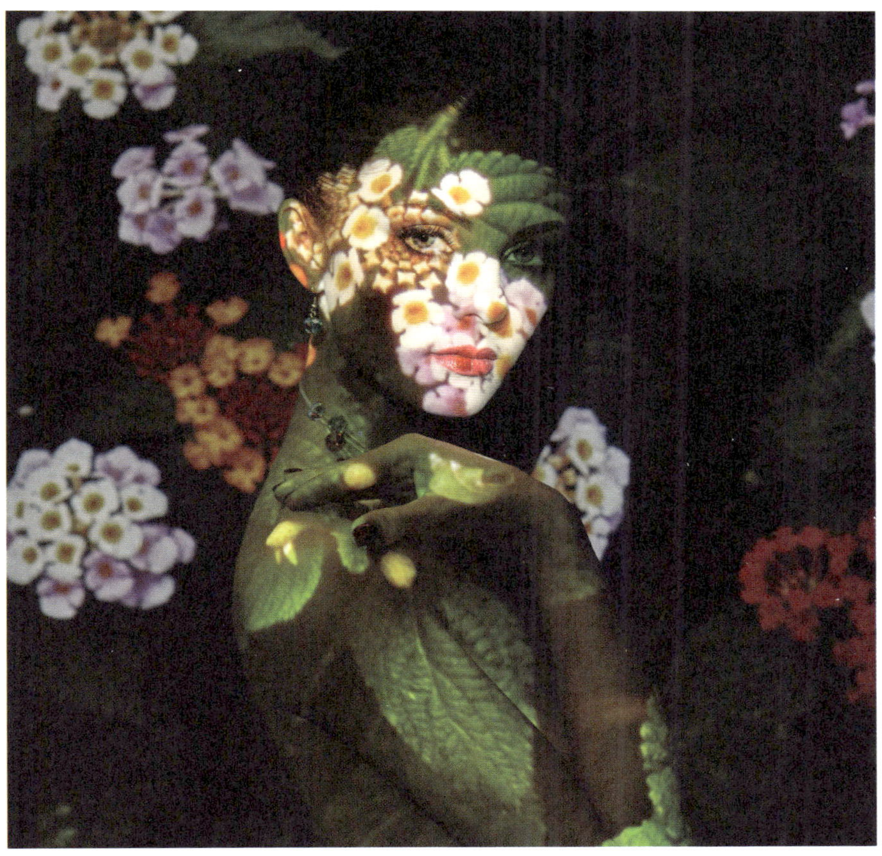

Projecting images such as flowers and patterns onto models can create
an inexpensive and extensive wardrobe, as well as dazzling effects.

ASSIGNMENT JOURNAL

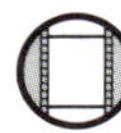

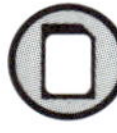

KIT LIST

- Item to freeze
- Freezer-proof container (ideally transparent)
- Freezer

TIPS

- You can shoot "top down" on your object to create a strong "record" shot of it, but also experiment with different angles, tighter crops, and shallow depth of field.

- Try adding a small amount of paint, ink, or food coloring to your water to tint the ice.

- Colored backgrounds behind the ice can help to add color.

- Don't forget to shoot at different melting stages as well. As the ice falls away different parts of your subject will start to appear, changing the way it looks.

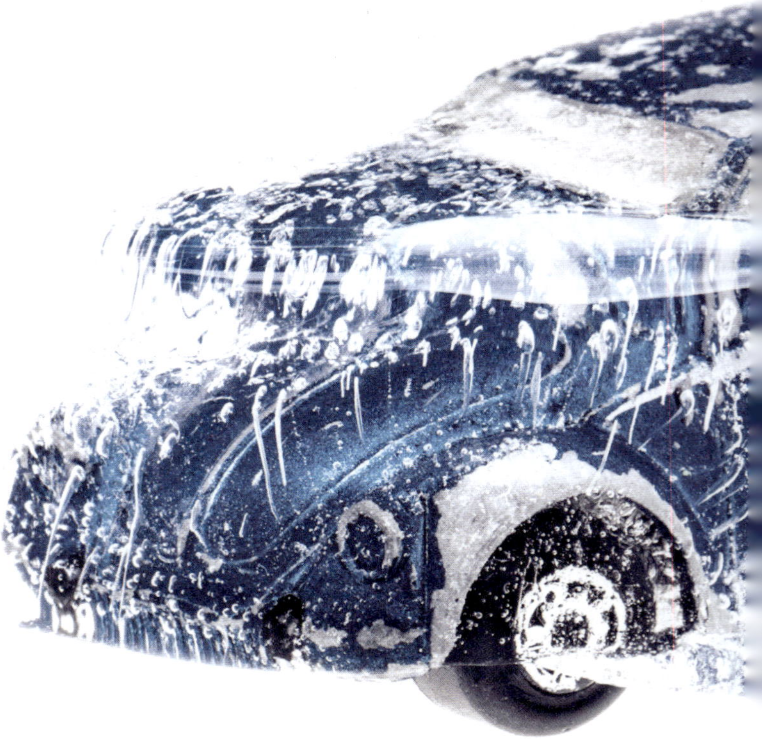

FREEZE FRAME

Putting objects in ice and photographing them is a really quick and easy way of transforming an otherwise "pedestrian" still life. All you need is a container to put your subject(s) in, some water, and a freezer. Once your subject is frozen you can either shoot it in the container, or tip it out and shoot it in the open—each option will create different shooting opportunities as the ice melts.

What you freeze is entirely up to you, but try to avoid hackneyed subjects such as leaves ("Look, it's winter!" has been done to death). Instead, explore alternative options and see if you can create something more than a record shot of an item in ice. Can you introduce some sort of narrative, for example? Maybe adding a print to the icy mix will help create a "story?" Always experiment, and try to take the basic idea as far as you can.

◄ *This toy car was left in a container of water in the freezer and then photographed at various points while it defrosted.*

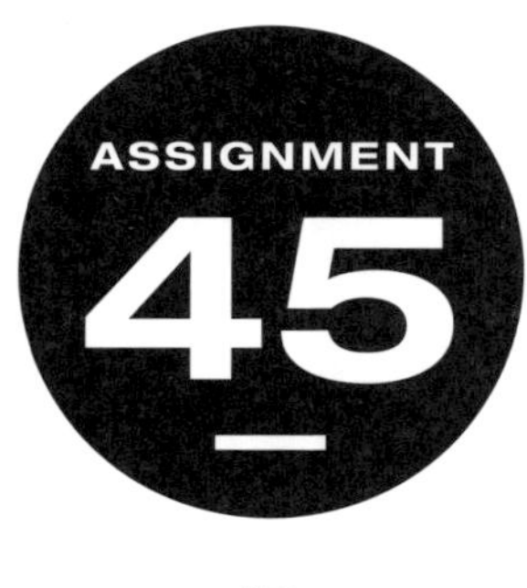

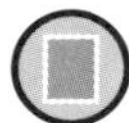

KIT LIST

- Laser print or photocopy (see Tips)
- PVA glue and foam brush (or similar)
- Material onto which image will be transferred
- Varnish (optional)

TIP

- Your transferred image will be reversed, so any writing in the original will be back-to-front unless you flip the image before you print it.

- Wood is a great receptor for this type of print transfer, but it's all about experimenting to see what works and what doesn't.

- Not all laser prints and photocopies will work successfully—it depends on the specific printer or copier you use, as well as the paper you print on (lighter weight papers are preferable).

SEE ALSO

- See how to transfer inkjet images in Assignment 04.

LASER TRANSFERS

Laser printers aren't great at giving you high-quality photo prints, but they can be used as the jump-off point to some creative transfer experiments.

1 Take a laser print and apply PVA glue to the image side of it, using a foam brush or similar. Place the print image-side down on a different material, such as wood. Leave the print for at least 24 hours to dry.

2 Once the glue is thoroughly dry, place it in a bowl of water to wet the paper. Now comes the difficult bit. You need to gently rub the paper to remove it—the glue and print should remain on your transfer material, while the paper gets rubbed away. The key is to take your time—you may need to repeat the process several times to get rid of all the paper residue, before leaving your transfer print to dry.

3 Coat the transferred image with varnish, or a similar clear coating to protect it.

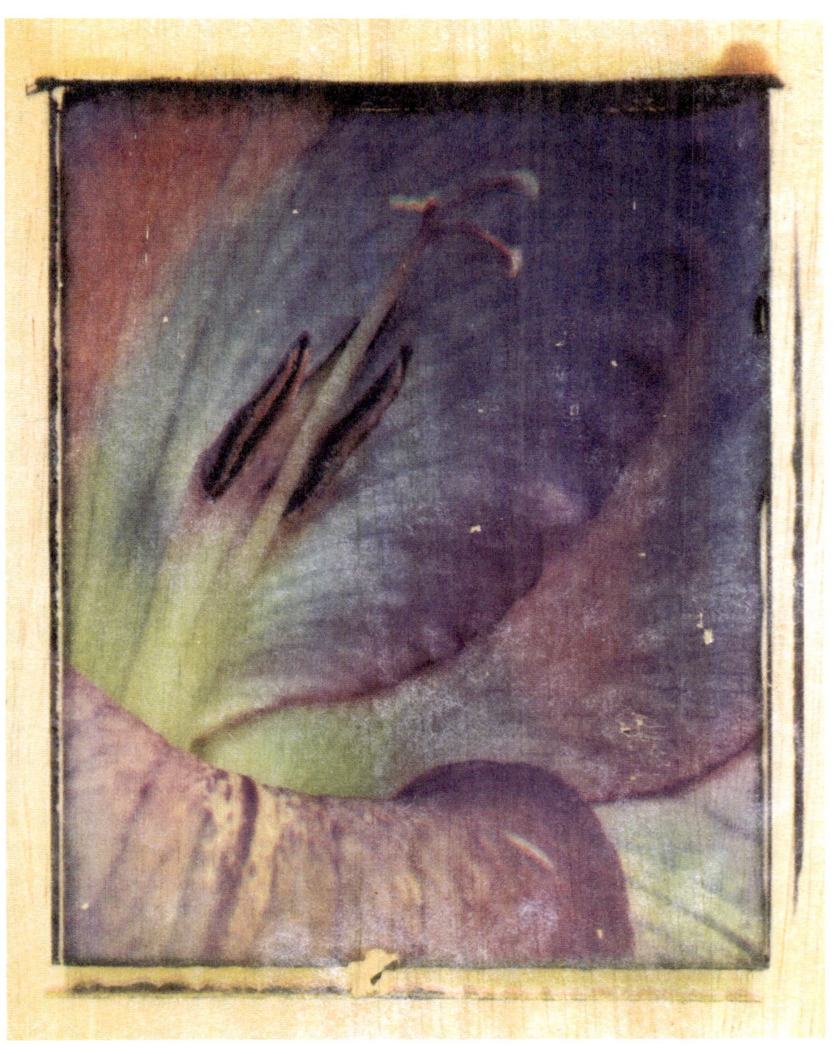

▲ The hardest part of a laser transfer is removing the paper without damaging the image too much. There's still some paper residue on this transfer, so it could probably do with another light wash. There are also a few "rubs" in the image, where it's been removed from the wood backing, but in moderation these add to the "handcrafted" appeal of the image.

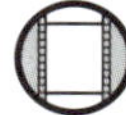

KIT LIST

- Medium-format Holga "toy" camera
- Film (120 roll film)

TIPS

- Although "Holagaramas" are intrinsically linked to Holga cameras, they can in fact be made using any medium-format camera that relies on you winding the film manually. However, unlike many cameras, a Holga makes the process incredibly straightforward.

- Always turn the camera from left to right: if you turn it in the other direction, your images will be exposed in the wrong order.

- The only limit to the number of shots in a Holgarama is the length of the film. You can have up to 16 overlapping frames if you really want (which would record two full 360-degree turns of the camera and give you an image almost 40 inches/1m long).

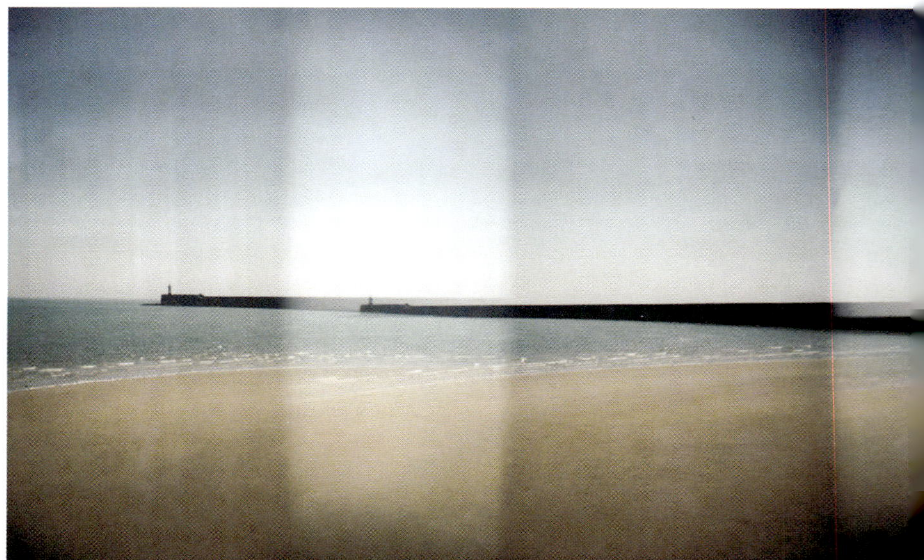

HOLGARAMAS

Medium-format Holga cameras (or "Holgas") first appeared in the early 1980s, but it took the advent of digital photography to propel them into the limelight. These ugly, primitive, and often flawed cameras are the perfect "lo-fi" analog antithesis of polished pixels, enabling you to shoot 6x6cm or 6x4.5cm format shots on regular 120 roll film. As many Holga-nistas have discovered, you can push the camera in a variety of more experimental directions, including the creation of "Holgaramas."

A Holgarama is simply a panoramic image made up of deliberately overlapping frames. Unlike a digitally created stitched panorama, no effort is made to seamlessly blend adjoining frames. Instead, there is a hazy overlap where the edge of one image is exposed over the top of the next. It's up to the viewer and his or her imagination to smooth things over.

▼ *Inconsistent overlaps and misaligned elements are part of a Holograma's DNA.*

THE (SHOOTING) PROCESS

1 The first thing to do is to make sure your Holga is set to shoot 6x6cm-format images, so remove the smaller 6x4.5cm mask if it's in the camera.

2 Although you are shooting 6x6cm images, set the frame-counter window to "16" (the setting for 6x4.5cm images). You'll see why in a minute...

3 Your first shot should be of the left edge of your intended Holgarama, so point your camera and shoot as you normally would with your Holga.

4 Wind on to the next frame, using the numbers on the film's backing paper. You're shooting 6x6cm in the camera, but winding on as if you're shooting 6x4.5cm images—the difference in the two formats is what creates the overlap between the frames.

5 Turn the camera to the right by roughly 45 degrees, using the viewfinder as a guide to keeping everything level. This should be enough to prevent any gaps appearing, or the overlaps from being too heavy.

6 Take a second shot. Wind on as before and turn the camera and shoot again if necessary. Stop shooting as soon as you reach the right edge of your intended Holgarama.

ASSIGNMENT JOURNAL

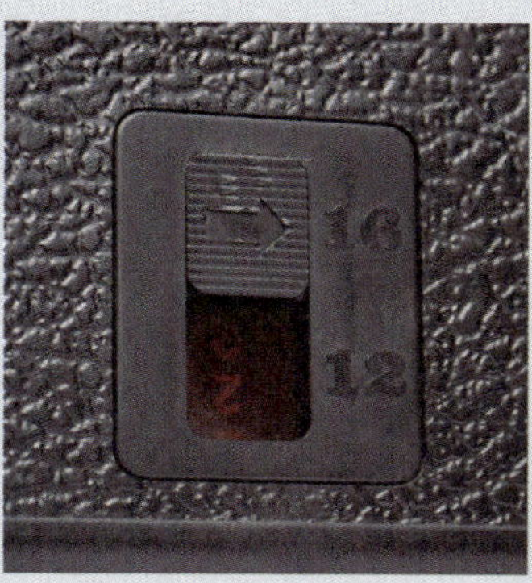

◄ *A key thing to remember is that you need to have the camera's wind-on window set to "16," so you are winding on as if you are shooting 6x4.5cm images.*

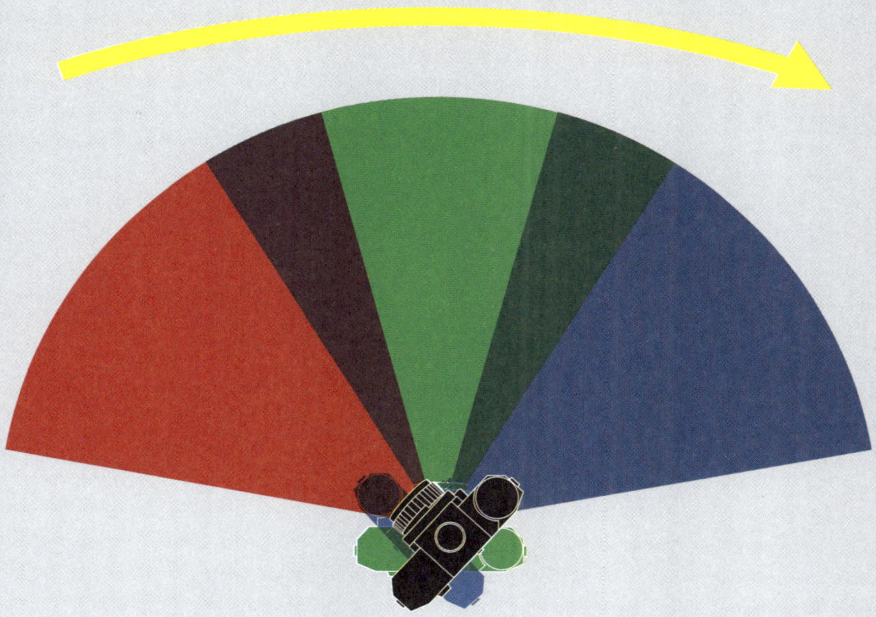

▲ *Always shoot your Holgaramas from left to right, turning roughly 45–50 degrees between shots.*

KIT LIST

- Film (exposed and processed)

TIPS

- If you're worried about permanently ruining your negatives, create a "texture roll" using a scrap film instead. Use bleach to remove the emulsion from a new, unexposed roll of film, so you're left with the clear plastic base. Paint and scratch onto it to add texture and then sandwich it with your images before printing or scanning.

- Experiment with color as well as black-and-white film, and slides as well as negatives.

SEE ALSO

If you want to preserve your film, you can also "attack" your prints (Assignment 14 and Assignment 29).

DISTRESSED NEGS

This experiment is all about celebrating the fragility and tactility of film by deliberately distressing its delicate surface. Take a roll of exposed and processed film (black-and-white is the perfect start point) and see how you can mark it. Scratch it, bleach it, or use heat to burn and blister it. Paint it, throw ink at it, or add (tiny) handwritten text. The name of the game is to explore how you can intentionally exploit the film itself to distress your images.

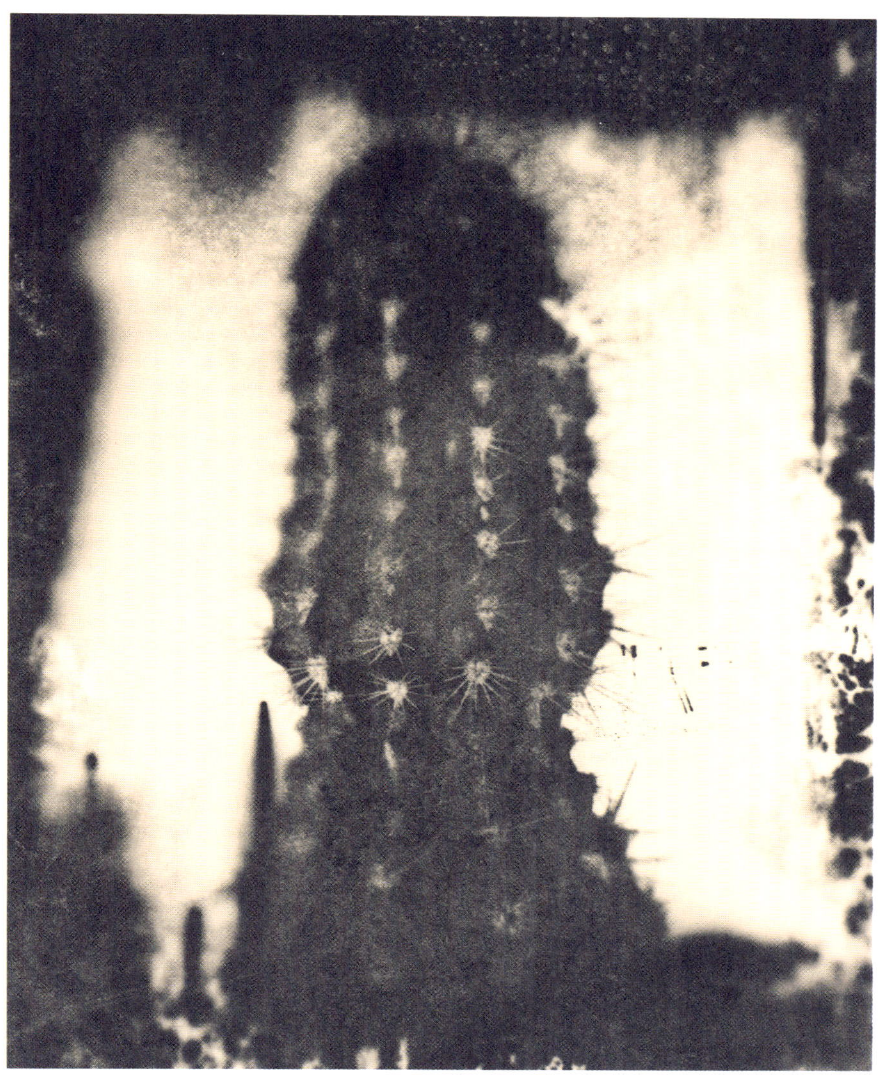

▲ *This simple photograph of a cactus was augmented by scratching, painting, and even burning the edges of the negative to "erode" the image.*

WARNING

This process is (usually) irreversible, so be aware that, if it goes wrong, you'll lose your negatives!

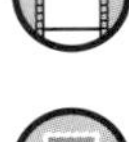

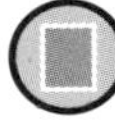

KIT LIST

- Black-and-white negative
- Traditional printing paper
- Darkroom
- Scanner (optional)

TIPS

- Paper negatives can be created using your computer and printer, but getting a print with dense blacks can be tricky: stacking two or more identical prints is one option.

- Use a pencil or ink to draw on the back of your paper negs: shading certain areas will lighten them in your final print.

- Make your prints on lightweight, fiber-based printing paper and then oil the paper (using olive oil or regular cooking oil) to make it more translucent. This will create a "thinner" negative to print from.

PAPER NEGS

The plastic base of photographic film is designed to give you the sharpest possible image, which is great if that's what you're after. Sometimes, though, you might want to create something a little softer, slightly more atmospheric, and possibly even textured. Although you can do all of that on your computer, it doesn't match the "hands on" fun of working with paper negatives.

There are several ways of creating paper negatives, but the two main options require access to a photographic darkroom. The first option (which is a common approach with homemade pinhole cameras) is to shoot using paper instead of film. You will need to experiment to work out the ISO (this may be in the region of ISO 5 or less), but the advantage is that once you've made your exposure and processed the paper, you've got your paper negative.

The second option starts with a regular film-based, black-and-white negative and is described on the following page.

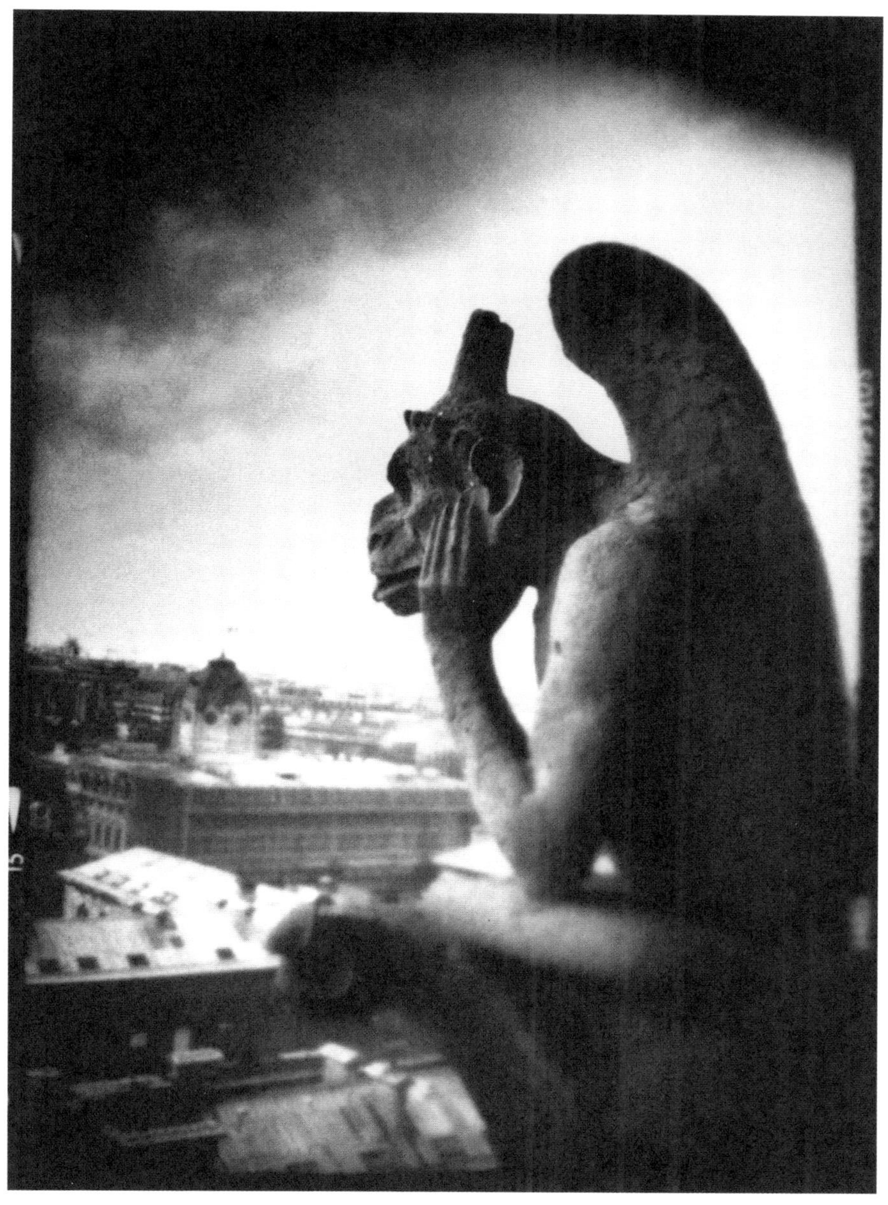

▲ *This image was shot on a vintage 6x9cm folding camera (on film), and then made into a paper negative using "Method 1" on the following page, so it could be enlarged and printed.*

The darkroom provides you with numerous ways of getting from a positive to a negative image, but there are two methods covered here: the first creates a small-scale paper negative that can be used in an enlarger instead of film (giving an "enlarged" paper texture); the second creates a larger negative for contact printing (ideal for solargrams and minimizing the paper texture). Experiment with both, depending on your goal.

THE PROCESS (METHOD 1)

1   Take your film negative and contact print it onto your photo paper. Develop and dry the print as normal so you have a same-size positive image on the paper.

2   Contact print your paper positive onto a second piece of photo paper to create a same-size paper negative to print from in your enlarger (or scan).

THE PROCESS (METHOD 2)

1   Take your film negative, put it in your enlarger, and print it normally to create a large positive print.

2   Contact print your paper positive onto a second piece of photo paper to create an enlarged paper negative. You can use your enlarged negative to contact print from (or scan).

SEE ALSO

Paper negatives are not just the start point for textured prints—you can also use them to create pictorial solargrams (Assignment 51).

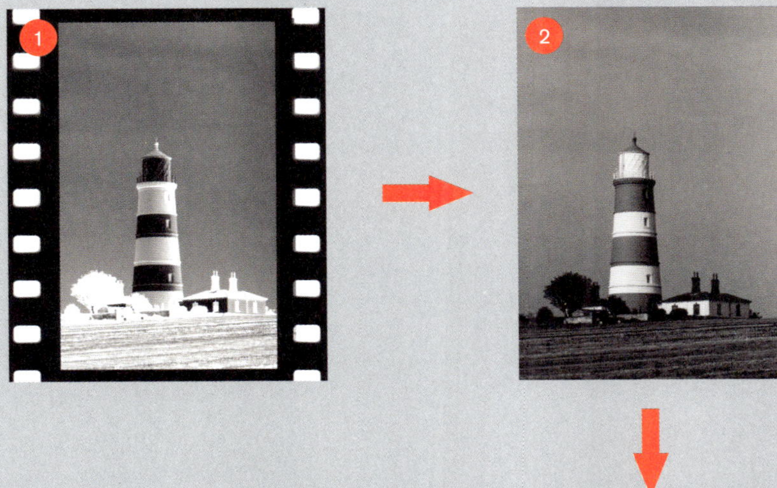

► *The steps in making a paper negative are broadly the same, no matter which method you use: a film negative (1) is used to make a paper positive (2), from which you make your textured paper negative (3). The only difference between the two methods is the stage at which you enlarge the image.*

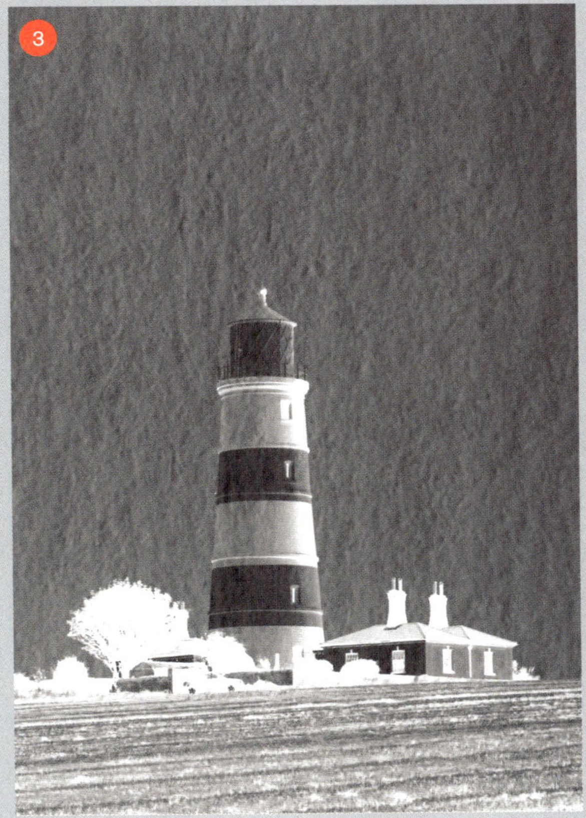

KIT LIST

- Prints
- Paint, ink, bleach—experiment!

TIPS

- You can work on black-and-white or color prints—adding color to a black-and-white shot is particularly striking, though.

- Your prints can be made traditionally or digitally, although this might affect what you can do to it. Bleach might react differently with a traditional darkroom print than it does with an inkjet print, for example (but try both and see!).

SEE ALSO

Don't confuse this experiment with color-popping (Assignment 16): this is about expressive mark-making, not "coloring in" part of a picture!

SPLASH OF COLOR

Sometimes it's good to be a little less predictable with your photography and a little less precious about your prints. So, cut loose! Splatter a print with angry, red paint to darken the tone; spray bleach to eat into the surface; allow ink to run down the paper, or "attack" with anything else you can think of.

This hands-on experiment is all about celebrating random marks, rather than thinking too carefully and precisely about what you're doing, so go wild! Have fun, channel your inner Jackson Pollock, and see where this free-flowing experiment takes you.

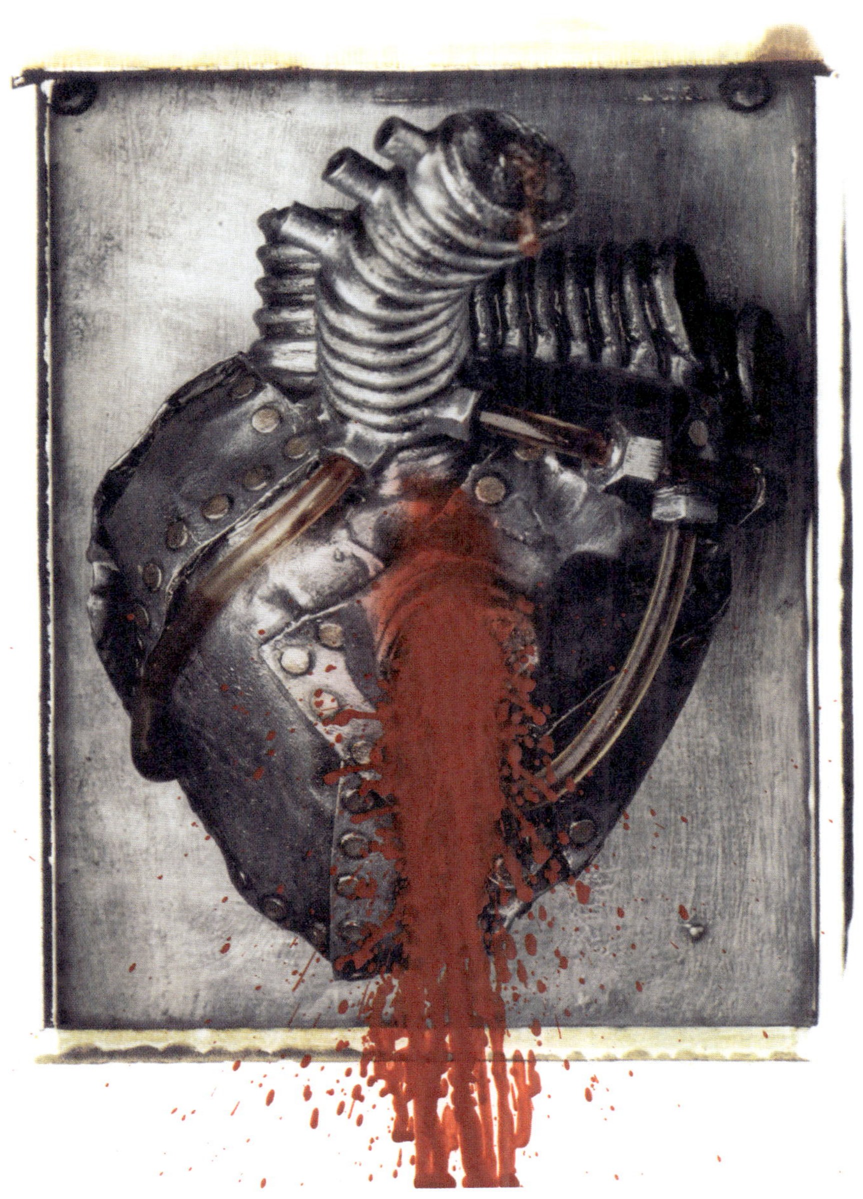

▲ *This model of a heart was made out of empty beer cans, clear pipe, and fake blood. I had a print made of it, which I stuck to a wall and sprayed heavily with red paint, allowing the paint to run down the page.*

KIT LIST

- Any type of camera (including cameraphone)

TIPS

- Don't just crop a single image into three—that's the easy way out!

- Think about the proportions of your three shots. Your wings don't have to be as tall as your central image, nor do they have to be narrower—experiment with different combinations.

- Assemble your triptych in your image-editing software if you want to print it as a single image.

- Don't just work horizontally—maybe a vertical triptych would best suit your subject?

POWER OF THREE

In photography, three is definitely a "magic" number—it's the driving force behind the rule of thirds, and is also the number that underpins solid triangular compositions. It's also been used widely in religious art in the form of "triptychs"—paintings in three sections, consisting of a larger central image and two smaller "wings" that add to the story of the composition.

This experiment is all about shooting in threes to create a single narrative. How you shoot and what you shoot is entirely up to you: the main thing is to think about how your shots work together in terms of size, shape, content, and—just as importantly—how they tell a story.

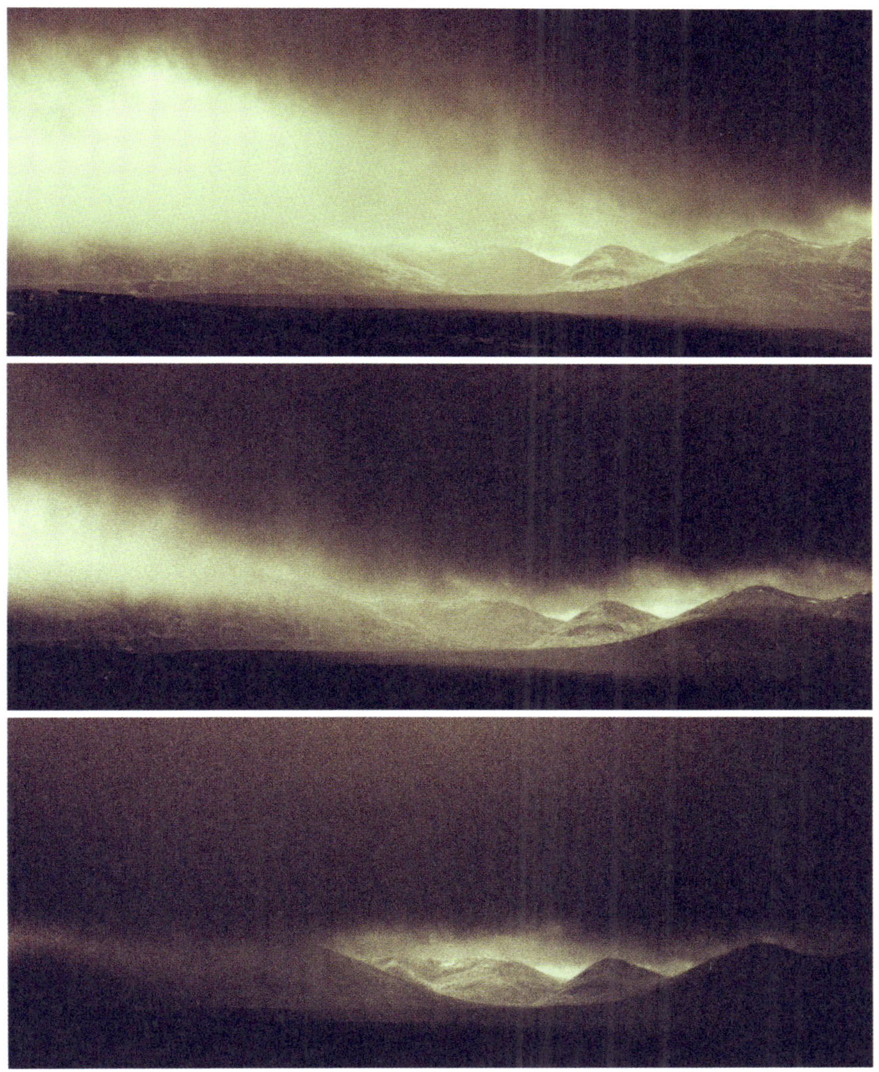

▲ *Three shots can enable you to show the passage of time using still images. This sequence shows the arrival of a storm and the "collapse" of the sky, creating a narrative with a clear beginning, middle, and end.*

51

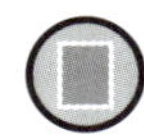

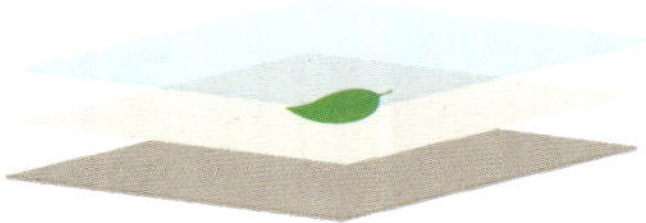

▲ *Holding your paper and subject flat together between a wooden board and a sheet of glass will give you the sharpest results.*

KIT LIST

- Sun print paper
- Clip frame
- Tray of water

TIPS

- Recognizable graphic subjects tend to work best for solargrams, as the process reduces tone and detail (much like shooting silhouettes).

- If you get really keen, you can mix your own cyanotype emulsion and use that to coat paper, fabric, or other surfaces you want to print on.

- A contact printing frame can be used instead of a clip frame, or you can use a simple card and glass "sandwich" instead.

- You don't need strong sunlight for a solargram (the process works using UV light), but the more overcast it is, the longer the exposure will be.

SEE ALSO

If you don't have a large-format camera, you can also create pictorial solargrams from paper negatives (Assignment 48).

SOLARGRAMS

Solargrams—also known as sun prints, cyanotypes, or blue prints—are created using one of the oldest photographic print processes, and they are one of the easiest to start experimenting with. The great thing about them is that—unlike a lot of traditional processes—you don't need a fully equipped darkroom. In fact, all you need is daylight to make your exposures (it will work on overcast days as well as sunny ones) and some plain water to develop your print in.

For your experiments you can explore lots of different ways of creating solargrams, from placing objects directly on the paper (to create silhouette-like photograms) to using negatives for a pictorial result (although bear in mind that these will be "same size" prints, so you may want to use medium- or large-format negatives, rather than 35mm). In both cases, the process is the same, as outlined here.

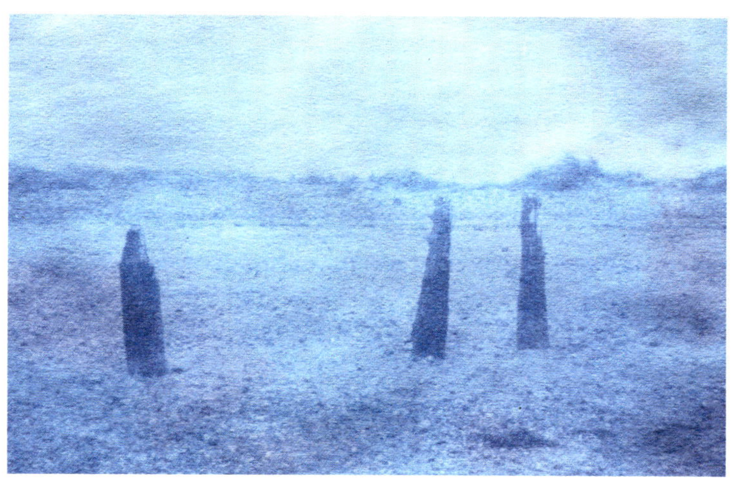

▲ *Cyanotypes get their name from their distinctive blue color, which is also where the term "blueprint" comes from. This one was made from a 6x9cm medium-format negative.*

THE PROCESS

1   You need to load your paper in low light, so do it indoors in a dimly lit room or in deep shade. Start by placing your sun print paper on the backing board of a clip frame.

2   If you're going to print a flat subject (such as flowers or a negative image on film or paper), place this on top of the sun print paper and fix the glass to the frame. This will stop the paper and subject moving around. Now jump to step 4...

3   If you're printing a three-dimensional object, you won't be able to close the frame, so pin your paper to the backing board to keep it still and place your item on top.

4   Take your frame outside into the light and put it down while the exposure is made. This can take a while (often minutes), depending on the paper you're using and the intensity of the light—follow the instructions on the paper, or use trial and error to get things right.

5   When your exposure's been made, quickly wash the paper in water. This will simultaneously end the exposure, develop the print, and wash it. You'll need to wash it for a minute or so before hanging your processed solargram up to dry.

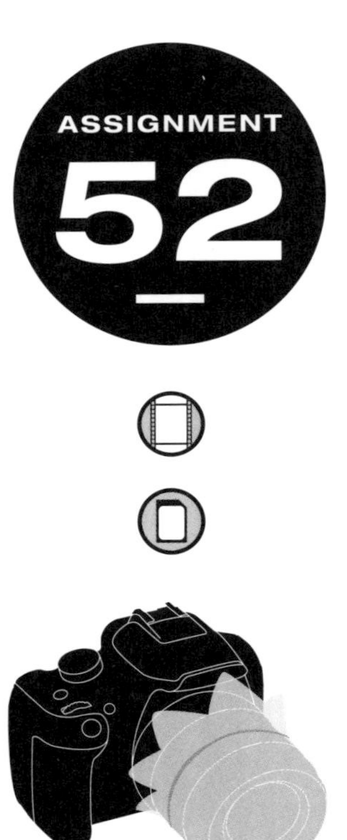

▲ *For this soft-focus filter I used a light, white fabric and stretched it over the lens hood.*

KIT LIST

- Any type of camera (including cameraphone)
- Pantyhose or stockings (or similar fabric)
- Rubber band

TIPS

- Experiment with different-colored nylons to see what effect color has on your images. You can also experiment with the "denier" (weight) as well.

- A classic alternative to pantyhose is to use petroleum jelly. However, don't apply it directly to the lens, as it's a nightmare to clean off. Instead, smear a small amount on an old UV filter—you can then fit the filter to your lens, or hold it in front of your lens if it doesn't have a filter thread.

SEE ALSO

Assignment 20 shows how you can selectively soften your images using plastic wrap; or you can defocus them instead (Assignment 01).

SHOOT SOFT

In the early days of Hollywood it was pretty much de rigueur to "soften" shots of the leading lady in a movie, so any slight imperfections disappeared and the star appeared to glow. Yet, despite being closely associated with black-and-white movies of the 1920s to 40s, the technique originated with pictorialist photographers such as Alfred Stieglitz and Edward Steichen—and now's the time to reclaim it.

Although you can buy specialist "soft-focus" portrait lenses, a far more cost-effective option is to stretch pantyhose (or stockings) across the camera lens to diffuse your shots. So, for this experiment, cut up some hose, attach it to your camera, and take a trip into the past by "shooting soft." Don't restrict yourself to female subjects and black-and-white images (like those early movie moguls). Stieglitz and Steichen both experimented with other subjects, as well as early color processes.

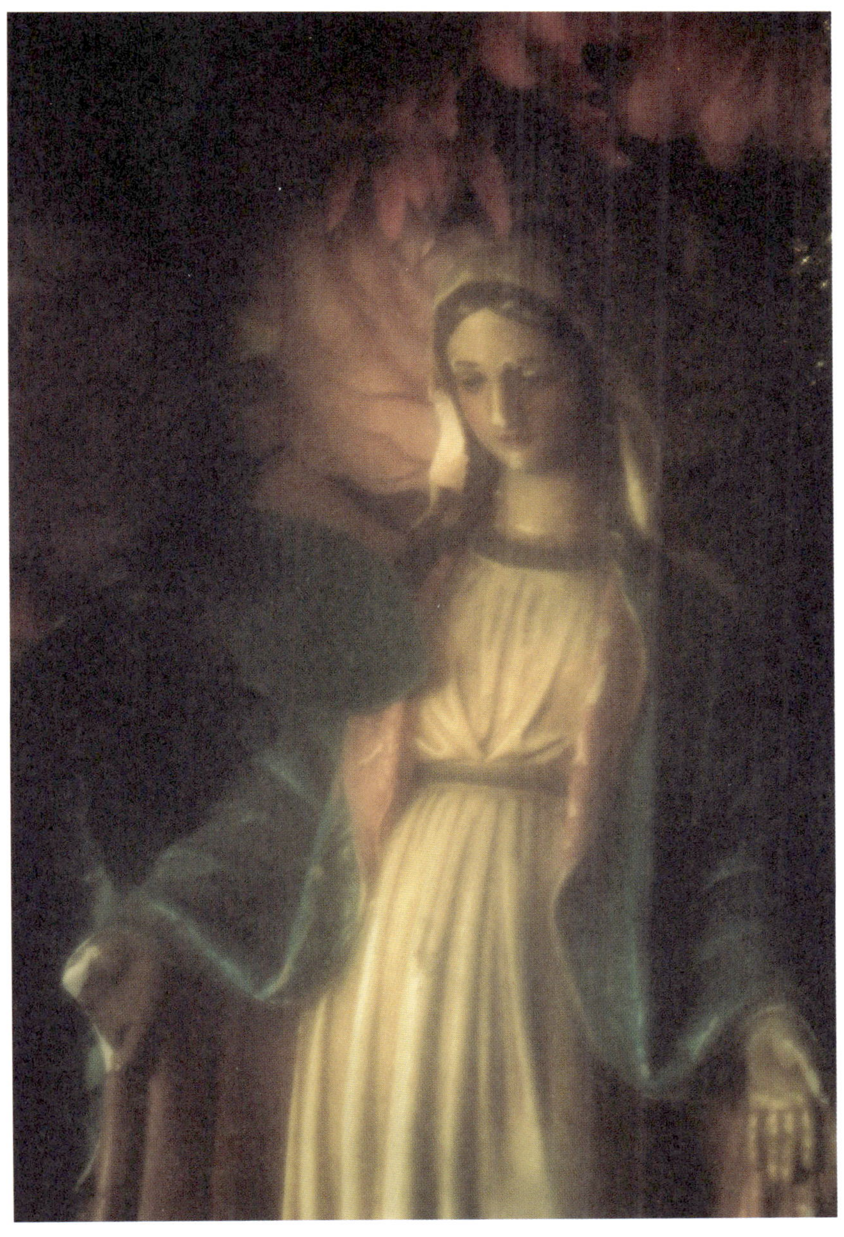

▲ *The filter shown here has had an obvious effect on this image, giving the figure a soft "glow."*

INDEX

First published 2018 by
Ammonite Press
an imprint of Guild of Master Craftsman Publications Ltd
Castle Place, 166 High Street, Lewes, East Sussex, BN7 1XU,
United Kingdom
www.ammonitepress.com

Reprinted 2022

ISBN 978 1 78145 354 4

Publisher: Jason Hook
Design Manager: Robin Shields
Designer: Luke Herriott
Editor: Rob Yarham

Color reproduction by GMC Reprographics

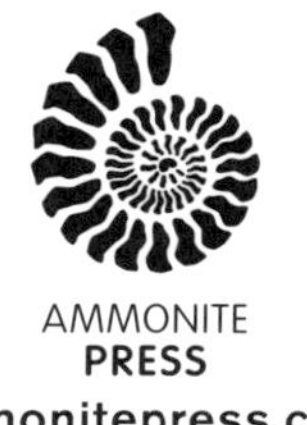

AMMONITE
PRESS
ammonitepress.com